How To Dress For Success In Midlife

NICOLE MÖLDERS

ISBN-13: 978-1537376950
ISBN-10: 1537376950

DEDICATION

This book is dedicated to my husband and photographer, Gerhard Kramm.

CONTENTS

ACKNOWLEDGMENTS

I thank foremost Dr. Gerhard Kramm for his patience in taking the photos and his encouragement to write this book. I wish to thank Judith Triplehorn and the Creative Space Team for their knowledgeable support and advice related to publishing. My gratitude also goes to the University of Alaska Fairbanks' Collegiate Society of Women Engineers, the University of Alaska Women Association, the University of Alaska Fairbanks Summer Sessions, the University of Alaska Fairbanks Office of Diversity, my fellow fashion and style bloggers, and the readers of *High Latitude Style* for fruitful discussion and helpful comments. Some outfit photos may include items of my choice that were sent to me by brands in exchange for writing and publishing a review post on my blog.

FOREWORD

In 2014, the University of Alaska Fairbanks' Collegiate Society of Women Engineers invited me to talk about "Dress for Success" within the framework of their guest lecture series. When preparing my talk I came across very interesting things about work appropriate dressing in various fields as well as for various life situations for women of any age. I have shared some of them on my blog *High Latitude Style* in a series called *Dress for Success*. This book includes some of the material that I collected and curated for the talk and these posts, but goes far beyond by providing additional material not presented on the blog or elsewhere.

The goal of this book help women in midlife to master any style situation with success including making a comeback into the work force. The book provides outfit inspirations for various dressing situations at work, when meeting family and friends, on holidays, and for special events in the community. In contrast to many other books on fashion and style, the application of the material, i.e. getting dressed for success in any midlife situation in a short time is in the foreground.

Like in a dictionary where you look up the meaning of a word, this book permits you to look up what you need to master your dressing situation. In addition, it discusses various aspects of the dressing situations, provides outfit suggestions and visual inspiration as well as information what to avoid and why. The outfit suggestions are not meant to recreate the look with items from your own closet, but to inspire and provide "recipes" for a suitable outfit.

The material is grouped into four chapters that focus on work related style situations including getting into the work force or getting a new job, family life and friends, holidays, and various social events in the community with various specific dressing situations in mind. As a dressing situation arises, you can restrict your reading to the general remarks at the beginning of the respective chapter plus the section that addresses the specific outfit occasion. When additional aspects might be of relevance and/or importance, the specific section has referrals to the sections that cover the additional material. This concept avoids repetition – in case you read the book cover to cover - and is meant as a time saver for the busy midlife woman of today. Think of the section of this book as your *cheat sheets to dress for success in midlife*.

This book is for all women in midlife who want to start to look to their best ever. It will help midlife women who enter a new phase in life, family, and/or professional wise, and women who have to learn to dress for their body changes related to menopause, as well as women who want to escape their about two decades old *style rut* of mommy jeans plus sweater.

I hope this book can be your smart *short-cut* to turn fashion into *Ageless Style*, and to master every style situation that midlife throws at you. Enjoy your book, fashion and style, and dress for success in midlife to your best ever.

Nicole Mölders,
Blogger at *High Latitude Style*
http://www.highlatitudestyle.com

Fairbanks, September 2016

1 Dress for Work and Alike

There is no *dress code* as tricky as *business attire*. However, it is nowhere so important to dress for success than for getting a job and advancing the career. Wearing the wrong and/or an *old-fashioned* outfit conveys the message that the wearer is *not on top of things*. The latter is not a promotional bell ringer in any job situation. Even the advice "dress for the position you want, not for the position you have," may be dangerous. Your (potential) boss may feel threatened by your following of that advice. Thus, dressing for job interviews, work and related businesses like conferences, workshops, trainings, and meetings is a balancing act that requires serious thoughts and considerations.

Additional difficulties related to *business attire* are that what is or is not work appropriate differs among work fields. In some fields, it means a three-piece suit, in others shirt, skirt/pants and blazer, i.e. *business casual* (**Outfits 1.1**, **1.2**). It may even differ in the same work field among work places, by geographic location, the seasons and among climate regions. Physical sciences, for instance, are work fields with the most casual work outfits, unfortunately, also the least fashionable ones. Creative job fields not only cover the classic arts, but also fashion sales persons as well as fashion and beauty related service fields. While employees in these fields have some freedom in expressing their individual style when dressing for work there are still limits.

The local climate may dictate that woolen tights and boots have to be accepted as work appropriate for the health of the employees. In summer, work places without air conditioning permit lighter clothes than those that have good air conditioning. Common sense with respect to the thermal comfort, however, may not always be the best adviser.

In this chapter, I provide suggestions how to navigate the minefield of *business attire* and to develop an understanding and judgement of what works and what does not for your office/job related situations. I provide the reasons for the given style/dressing suggestions to enable you to learn how to *dress for success* and master any style situation.

Historically and still today, a *dress code* is all about expectations. Customers have an expectation regarding the firm and their employees. Thus, especially in male dominated fields, the customers expect a guy to show up. Depending on the field, he would come dressed in a suit, shirt with a tie, polished shoes, schlepping a leather briefcase and would look like a business man when it is about selling services/consulting, or dressed in an overall when it is about repair, add a hard-hat for construction and alike. The respective outfit depends on the products and/or services their employer provides.

Outfit 1.1. Business casual attire   **Outfit 1.2.** Business casual attire

You know yourself that you only have one chance to make a first impression. By being female in a male dominated field, you already fail to meet the first expectation. The same applies when you just finished your degree after being a stay-at-home mom for 20 years, and they expect a twenty something to show up. Therefore, it is very important to meet all other expectations of the potential employer or client and not to lose any further brownie points than being female over 40.

1.1 Job Interview

An invitation to a job interview means you made the short list, but you are not quite there. Depending on the field companies invite up to four candidates for onsite interviews.

For success in the interview take control when and where you have the possibility to do so. Your outfit is in your control. Let us assume you applied for a job in a more conservative field. On one hand side, your goal is to create a polished, classic outfit that conveys the message "I know what I am doing, I take charge and control, I am a professional." However, on the other hand side, you also want to send the message that you are on top of things, i.e. up-to-date. These goals sound controversy and like squaring the circle.

When the company has a webpage with photos of their employees browse it to see what they are wearing. This research is a good start to find the bar that you should up a notch. Err on the most formal side of their wardrobe.

Go for sober neutrals (gray, navy, black, tan, brown) and a pop of color in your top or accessories (scarf, bag, belt, necklace). Stay away from anything beige or graige. The former color looks *old*, the latter looks *dirty*. Both attributes are adverse to your goal to land the job.

For young women a suit reads "I am mature." Once you are over 40, a skirt or pants suit may work in your disadvantage as it reads "I am conservative." The suit makes you look *old* and/or conveys the message that you might live in the past. Given the ageism of today's society and the fast pace of work technology, you cannot afford to appear either *old* or not being up-to-date. A work dress (**Outfit 1.3**) or a combination of blazer and skirt (**Outfit 1.4**) or blazer and pants (**Outfits 1.1., 1.2**) feel more modern, *fashion-forward* and conveys that you stayed *young* and *hip* even though you graduated from high school more than 20 years ago.

When wearing pants stay away from tapered pants unless you have very thin hips. Tapered pants add bulk around your hips and may give a wrong impression about your health and/or weight and (work) activity. Remember that many people have the incorrect perception that heavy people are lazy and/or slow.

Go for closed toe pumps with heels even in summer. In many conservative fields, sling backs, open-toe pumps and/or sandals are a *no-no*. Pointy toe pumps are too sexy for an interview in a conservative field. Pumps with heels of about 2.5 inch (5 cm) or so look professional. The so-called court pumps – think Kate Middleton's pumps – are a safe bet. When you like to add some height, get pumps with an insole, and/or with a slightly thick sole of 2/5 inch (1 cm) at most. When you are not used to walking in heels opt for wedges and exercise walking in them. They give more stability than pumps and are easier to walk in.

Never wear brand new shoes to an interview. You may get a site tour and you may end up with blisters in the best case. In the worst case, you start limping and are visually in pain, which may lead to wrong conclusions about your health and endurance. It also could convey the message that you are unrealistic and unprepared for the tasks at hands, which in this case was the task to visit the site.

Add a structured bag that is big enough to hold a tablet, lap top and folder as well as all the other things that you typically have in your bag. This size conveys the message that you are prepared and willing to take work home if needed.

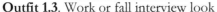

Outfit 1.3. Work or fall interview look   **Outfit 1.4**. Work/interview look

You should strive to convey the message that you pay attention to details. Unless they give you a task to show what you can do, the only way to demonstrate that you care for details is showing that you take care of yourself. Get a manicure on the day before your interview as you have to have your hands on the table. The future boss and/or colleagues on the search committee will sit just a yard or so in front of you. Thus, have your eye brows done the day before as well.

Your makeup should be barely there, but at the same time, it should be clearly visible that you applied makeup. It is a balancing act. The goal is to look professional, and not like going out, "I don't care" or "I am here for men hunting."

Get a nice haircut a week before the interview. By the time of your interview your hair looks not like you just came from the hair dresser. So to speak it looks more *normal*. Your hair should fall naturally, look clean and healthy. Thus, use hair spray sparsely, if at all. When time permits, get a blowout prior to going to the interview, but ensure they don't overdo it.

When you dye your hair, make sure roots are not showing. Have a root touch-up the day before the interview or use root cover-up spray. Gray hair should not look yellowish, i.e. blue it if needed. Make sure your hair is not hiding your face. A face hidden by hair may be conceived as being insecure or too flirty.

Make sure your clothes and accessories are flawless (no spots, runners, knots, open seams, wrinkles, no distress on bags or shoes, no heel damage, etc.). Your shoes should look polished. Having a spare pair of pantyhose in your bag will give you some peace of mind. I once needed them and was happy to have a spare pair in my purse. A runner never meets the *dress code*.

The more conservative the potential workplace is, the more conservative you should go with the choice of your jewelry. However, keep your jewelry in the contemporary field. Gold or silver colored items are great. Studs are best, as they do not make noise when you are on a phone. Choose classic styles in gold for the most authority. Avoid large earrings if you are in very traditional, conservative fields like finance and law. In executive dressing, dangly or hoop earrings are a *no-no*.

A pearl necklace is sort of the equivalent to the men's tie. However, stay away from wearing pearl studs and a pearl necklace at the same time once you are over 40. Matching jewelry was a thing in the Sixties. Thus, it reads *old-fashioned*. The latter can be mistaken as not being up-to-date. Instead of pearl studs, go for diamond studs (fake or real) with the pearl necklace.

Keep the arm party at home as the binging and banging of the bangles cause noise. Noise is unwanted in cubicle areas or shared offices. Moreover, it may be annoying and/or come across as disrespectful in an interview.

Wear a functioning watch to convey the message that you take time (deadlines) seriously. It doesn't matter that you check the time on your cell phone. I do it too, despite I wear a watch on a regular basis. Switch your phone off shortly before going into the interview. The vibration setting is not an option as a vibrating phone in a bag may become embarrassing.

There is no need to run to the department store for a complete head-to-toe new outfit. Shop your own closet for classic and current items first and add as needed. Here are some basic outfit suggestions including options for swaps:

- Pencil skirt around knee-length or wide leg pants (read not skinnies, but not Marlene Dietrich pants either) in a neutral color, blazer in another neutral color, court pumps (i.e. round toe pumps), silky shell with sleeves or blouse, contemporary bracelet/bangle, brooch or necklace as finishing touch

- For an all season classic *business attire* look: Navy blue blazer with gold metal buttons, gray pencil skirt, chambray or white button-down shirt, pearls, court pumps or gray or navy dress shoes or multi-metallic pumps (more modern vibe), modern print scarf (to dial down the conservative component), multi-compartments structured leather bag for lap top or tablet (A briefcase would look *over the top* at an interview.)

- For a winter *American classic* outfit, i.e. *business casual dress code*: Tweed skirt, blazer, chambray or white button-down shirt, heeled loafers (nasty weather) or court pumps, statement necklace or pearl necklace

- Tailored dress that flows over your body, short suit jacket, court pumps, modern scarf or medium long necklace

- Culottes (when in fashion), blazer, simple top, pearl necklace, diamond studs, watch, structured bag, court pumps

- Classic tailored solid neutral color or classic pattern (e.g. pinstripes) dress, pumps, brooch, structured bag (**Outfit 1.3**)

- Black/neutral color straight or pencil skirt, neutral light color blazer, abstract print top, statement necklace or pearl necklace, court pumps

Here is some general advice:

1. Avoid dresses with floral prints or anything that is *girly* or very feminine (e.g. lace).
2. Plaid may be risky unless it is in neutral colors and clearly not *punk* (**Outfits 1.3, 1.5**).
3. Add a matching belt when a dress, skirt or pants have belt loops.
4. Adapt the colors of the top to the respective season to look up-to-date and on top of things.
5. Remember, it is always better to be slightly overdressed than underdressed. Being overdressed is seen as respect, while the opposite conveys the message "I don't care."

Keep in mind when you enter the place, your outerwear is what they see first, and the first impression should be in your favor. When the weather requires outerwear, go for classic coats like a trench coat, camel coat, or pea coat. A nice cashmere or silk scarf is always a great investment.

The choice of your outerwear depends on the weather and season. You don't want to show up wetted by rain, or in season-inappropriate clothing. Both would convey the message that you are *unrealistic*.

Therefore, check the forecast issued by the closest local National Weather Forecast office. When rain is in the forecast, have an umbrella handy. There are nice folding umbrellas small enough to fit into your large bag. Use the umbrella, if needed. You don't want to enter totally wet and with a ruined blowout. Instead you want to enter dry with a wet umbrella conveying the message "I am on top of things and stay the weathers."

A good choice for windy, rainy weather is a trench coat. Never belt a trench coat. If at all, tie it. However, to protect your indoor interview outfit from wrinkles do not tie the trench on the way to the interview. Keep the trench coat open when the weather allows for it with the belt knotted in the back. This look is the most stylish. When it rains or is windy just close the buttons.

In windy regions and/or fall, a cocoon leather coat (**Outfit 1.5**) is another great choice as outerwear. It is roomy enough so a dress or blazer underneath does not wrinkle. It also can take light rain. Thus, you look prepared for various weathers.

Outfit 1.5. Interview outerwear   **Outfit 1.6**. Interview outerwear

When your interview is in winter, you may need a hat. However, take the hat off before you enter the interview/conference room. It is part of being respectful! Make sure you choose a hat that will not leave you with a hat head or bed head when taken off. A bed head like Brigit Bardot is not an acceptable look at an interview. Berets are great options for women with curly and straight hair alike (**Outfit 1.6**). When you wear gloves, take them off as well. Only Queen Elizabeth greets people with her gloves on.

Like for the hat, never wear sunglasses in a job interview! When it is a sunny day and you needed sunglasses for driving to the location, take them off before going in. Do not shift them in your hair like you often do at the beach, when running errands or for style on weekends. Doing so would convey the message "I can't wait to get out of here to enjoy the sun."

Speaking of glasses. When you need reading glasses, have them in your bag, easily accessible. In plain English, you should not have to search for them when you need them. Do not hang the reading glasses around your neck on a reading-glass necklace. These necklaces convey the message that you forget where you put your glasses when you take them off. Who would hire a forgettable person? Also do not make the big mistake not to have them with you. When you have to read something and hold the paper away from you and/or squeeze your eyes to read, it will convey the message that you are not ready to work because of your eyesight. Who can afford to have an employee who orders 788 items due to the lack of reading glasses just because the one and the two zeros looked like a seven and two eights?

Outfit 1.7 works in the conservative field when swapping the leather pants and pointy toe pumps with slacks and court pumps, respectively. Wearing black or white slacks with a hounds tooth blazer and replacing the zebra top with a bright solid or black top makes **Outfit 1.8** suitable for the conservative field as well.

1.2 Job Interview in a Creative Field

All the points about neatness (makeup, grooming, wrinkle-free clothes, polished shoes, clean clothes, hair, etc.) brought up for the job interview in a conservative field (**Section 1.1**) apply to a job interview in a creative field as well. Here you want to convey the message that you are professional <u>and</u> creative, can fit in, but also can stand out. Thus, you pick an outfit under the same considerations as for a job interview in a conservative field, but a bit less *formal* to include the message that you are also creative.

To achieve this goal combine classic pieces with one item that shows your creativity. Here is how you can play this card out: In creative fields, black is always a good idea. Think of Isaac Mizrahi, Karl Lagerfeld, Jason Wu, just to mention a few.

A faux wrap dress with a fashion forward unexpected small print in neutral colors is a nice option for an interview in the creative field. The cut/style is conservative enough for serious business. Even the Duchesse of Cambridge wears wrap dresses. When wearing a wrap dress always opt for a faux one. You do not want to risk that the wind exposes your legs. Another advantage of a faux wrap dress is that your legs will remain covered when you sit and cross them.

A blazer in a bright color is a great statement piece (**Outfits 1.7, 1.10**). In the South in summer, a white blazer is a great option to avoid getting chicken bumps from über-active air conditioning during the interview.

In contrast to the conservative work field, you can sport open-toe pumps when it is appropriate for the weather and season. Wedge or heel ankle boots are great options too. Go for a statement belt or accessory. Leopard, zebra, giraffe or snake prints are great options for the belt, shoes or bag, but only one animal print at a time. When wearing a long (statement) necklace make sure that you always hold it back when sitting down. You do not want to cause noise with it or have it in the soup. Better, make sure it is short enough for this to happen.

Outfit 1.7. Interview creative field

Outfit 1.8. Interview creative field

Outfit 1.9. Interview creative field

Outfit 1.10. Interview creative field

Another creative statement are mixing prints and patterns, best in black and white with (**Outfits 1.7, 1.8**) or without (**Outfit 1.9**) a pop of color. Here are further outfit ideas for a job interview in a creative field:

- Black slim pants, tapered trousers, 3/4 pants, wide slack pants paired with a colorful or bright-colored solid shirt, may be with a camisole underneath, black pumps, neutral color (except black) bag
- Black pencil skirt, colorful printed blouse worn over the skirt, statement belt, large structured bag, black pumps, small studs
- In warm climate regions and/or summer: Solid color knee-length dress, pumps, bag in another color
- Printed or solid structured bag or pumps, solid colored dress, statement necklace

1.3 New Job

Being new on the job means you successfully mastered the interview dress challenges. You made the cut and got the job – congratulations! Getting the job is not where it stops to matter how you dress. There is a pinch of truth to the Swiss novelist Gottfried Keller's story "Kleider Machen Leute" (clothes make people). It is important how you dress for work. However, don't buy a whole new wardrobe prior to completing your first two weeks on the new job. You may end up with items you will never wear.

Instead wear your trusted classic items in outfits that are a little dressed down version of what you wore at the job interview (see **Sections 1.1, 1.2**). That outfit passed their *dress code* once, i.e. it was a winner. Thus, you cannot be wrong with variations of that outfit.

In the first two weeks, pay attention to what your most stylish and most successful colleagues are wearing as well as to what your boss wears. Identify their key items by answering these five questions.

1. Is there a *dress code*, and how close is it followed?
2. Is this a dress, pants, skirts, pants suit, skirt suit, or casual place?
3. Is there and if yes, what is the *Casual Friday* culture or *dress code*?
4. What are the brands and fabrics that are *It* among colleagues at same rank or one rank up?
5. What are the key items of what they wear at work that will work with your style/taste?

Use the answers to these questions as a guide to start a shopping list for your new work wardrobe. Use your phone to store the list so you have it always handy to take notes and/or check it when at the mall. Start shopping for the items that are missing in your "interview suitable wardrobe" to transfer it into a "work wardrobe" for the new job. Work from there down the list.

When creating your new work wardrobe make sure you stay true to yourself, i.e. your style. Avoid to be a *copy cat*. Just take the elements of the (written or unwritten) *dress code* as the skeleton to create a wardrobe that is *so you*. There are several reasons to do so. First of all, you feel more confident in your own skin when you wear what you like. This confidence will show, which will have a positive impact for your advancement on the job. Second, you convey the message that you have own ideas. Colleagues will more likely ask for your opinion or listen to what you have to say. Third, you don't look like wearing a uniform when there is no need to wear one. Even when you have to wear a real uniform, always try to style it as far as possible in a way that it reflects you.

The color or print of a top, a scarf, a statement necklace or belt, shoes, for instance, are good opportunities to introduce your style into your new work wardrobe. Here you may even have already pieces that you can use for your new job wardrobe. In creative fields or when the *work dress code* allows leather, you may consider suede and leather to give your style a little edge. Suede is a softer version of leather, but requires more care than leather. However, it is easier to get away with suede than leather at work.

Outfit 1.11. Unusual color combination   **Outfit 1.12**. Sheath w. orange bag

A faux twinset (sweater and cardigan of different color) is a clever way to look *polished*, but *fashion-forward* at work. Use mixing pattern (e.g. floral top and leopard print belt), modern color combinations (**Outfits 1.11**) to add an edge and individual style to work outfits for the conservative field. Note that leopard print and metallic are modern neutrals. Statement color choices (**Outfit 1.12**, **1.13**) can introduce/show off your individual style in the creative field. **Outfit 1.14** features a suede skirt with blazer, sweater, statement necklace and leopard pumps.

When your job does not include client visits outside of the building, i.e. your outerwear is not part of your work wear, you can go more wild with your style in this part of your wardrobe. Otherwise look for professional outerwear (see **Section 1.1** Job Interview). Tip: Below knee-length is advisable for skirts and dresses when the *dress code* calls for nude panty hose and prohibits opaque tights in winter.

Here are additional work outfit suggestions:

- Sheath dress in *dress code* appropriate hem length with sweater underneath for a winter office look in a cold climate region in the conservative field
- Sheath dress, fitted tweed blazer, pumps
- Dress, cardigan, opaque tights, loafers for a winter office look in the conservative field in cold climate regions

Outfit 1.13. Color block work dress   **Outfit 1.14**. Fake skirt suit

1.4 Engineering

In this section, "engineering" is used as a representative for a job in a male dominated field. Many of the suggestions given with respect to meeting with customers/clients also apply for business women, lawyers, real estate managers, travel agents and alike.

About 70% of the engineering work is meeting and working with clients. Most women engineers work in state, government, academia, clothing or food related fields where client contact is typically low. In many offices without customer contacts, wearing pants, a sweater and dress shoes, or skirts with a twinset and pumps are considered office appropriate (**Outfits 1.15, 1.16**).

Outfit 1.15. Winter work outfit

Outfit 1.16. Winter work outfit

While the *dress code* varies among engineering fields when doing the actual engineering work, it nails down to a quite similar *dress code* when it comes to meeting with clients like when interviewing for the position (see **Section 1.1** for outfit suggestions). In engineering like in business, meeting the *dress code* is so important that many top notch engineering schools even devote a web page and Pinterest board to *What to Wear*.

However, the suggestions provided for women are cookie-cutter outfits. Such boring looks risk conveying the (wrong) message of not being creative at all. The latter is not a promotional bell ringer for any job that is all about developing ideas and make them work like engineering, management, or business for instance.

A tailored pants suit is a great option for female engineers under 40. Once you are over 40 an unmatched pants suit works to your advantage. Swap the pointy toe pumps that usually are worn with a pants suit for oxfords with a sturdy, not clunky heel, not higher than 1.5 inch (3.75 cm). This heel height still allows climbing a ladder when you (unexpectedly) have to do so when meeting with customers of your firm. Wedges are a safer alternative than heeled oxfords. Another advantage of wedges is that you can go for a higher heel height than with low heel oxfords and still climb a ladder. You want to be eye height with the guys, no matter whether they are colleagues or customers.

Make sure the length of your pearl necklace is short enough to not get caught in machinery. That is the reason why male engineers wear tie holders. Get a men's watch to convey the message to your firm's customers that meeting deadlines and being on time is high priority. Another advantage of a men's watch is that you can read the time without your reading glasses. Cuff the sleeves of your blazer for style. Cuffed sleeves also convey the message that you are ready to get your hands dirty, i.e. do the job. Most importantly, learn how to stand like a man. The feet must be shoulder width apart and the toes should be directed slightly outside.

Get a big structured leather tote that can hold a laptop, iPad and a folder. It indicates that you are having the relevant paperwork with you and access to relevant documents and information at your finger tips to get the job done. If your field is about going outside very often, you should have the appropriate shoes (e.g. iron-capped boots, engineering boots, rubber boots), and hard hat in a tote either in your office or car.

Go with neutrals for the suit, shoes, and leather tote. Express your style by the choice of the blouse or shirt. The blouses should have no see-thru fabric. A turtleneck sweater in silk, cashmere or similar quality knit is a good alternative to a button-down shirt or blouse in cold climate regions and/or winter.

Wear a classic coat that is short enough to not hinder you to climb and/or pick something up (**Outfits 1.17, 1.18**). A pea-coat was designed – or should I say engineered – for climbing masts. The trench coat was designed to face the weathers in the trenches of the Great War. Thus, a short trench coat gives you the possibility to move and climb too. However, make sure to have the belt knotted in the back. It looks plain ridiculous when you bend down and the belt's tips dip in the mud. Note that one never belts a trench coat.

Wear nude non-opaque socks or socks that match the color of the pants and/or shoes. You still want the elongated legs, however, not only for style, but also for the illusion of looking taller than you actually are (unless you are already taller than most guys).

When you are more a skirt kind of gal, wear skirts on days where you expect to work at your desk or only meet customers in conference rooms. Nevertheless, as emergencies may occur, always have a neutral pair of wrinkle-free pants in the trunk of your car so you can change prior to driving to where ever you are needed.

When you go for a skirt, make sure it is wide enough to move. For instance, a straight skirt with a slit in the back that permits you to step up on low equipment or some steps of a ladder. In the choice of your skirt, steer clear away from side or front slits. They show too much leg when you sit. Moreover, the skirt should not ride up and it should still reach to your knees when sitting. Wide and/or long skirts are inappropriate for a woman engineer as they can get caught in moving equipment. They are a safety issue as are high heels.

Outfit 1.17. Work outerwear   **Outfit 1.18**. Work outerwear

Always wear bikers or shorts underneath your skirt so there is no embarrassing sight when you unexpectedly have to climb equipment or a ladder in your skirt. Check that the shorts/bikers don't show when you sit. In winter, opaque tights are a great option in cold climate regions.

When you have long hair, style it in such a way that a hard hat still will fit and that when taken off, your hair doesn't look like Brigitte Bardot's famous bedhead. A low sitting braid is a great option. A wavy shag is easy to manage with hard hats.

Outfits 1.1, **1.2**, and **1.17**, **1.18** are inspirations for work inside without customer meetings and stylish outerwear for meeting with customers outside, respectively. Here are further *business casual* outfit and outerwear suggestions:

- Navy blue blazer, gray straight pants, matching belt, chambray or white button-down shirt, pearl necklace, gray wedges or heeled oxfords

- Tweed or Irish plaid blazer, wool pants or slacks, chambray or white button-down shirt, low oxford lace-up heels, loafers or wedge heels in the color of the pants
- Dark neutral color straight pants, neutral light color blazer, abstract print top, short pearl necklace, wedges
- Pea-coat or duffle coat, scarf, hat when meeting with clients for a site inspection or inspection of work progress

1.5 Casual Friday

Many work places have some *Casual Friday* culture. Casual Friday still means that you have to look proper, clean and professional. In some offices, it may mean a clean pair of jeans with a dark wash and a quality T-shirt. In other offices, it may mean that you can wear jeans instead of the usual slacks or pants. In some university science departments with heavy focus on field work, Casual Friday may even mean that you dress up a notch, i.e. *Informal Friday*. In university settings, Fridays are often reserved for meetings and seminars.

Outfit 1.19. Casual Friday look   **Outfit 1.20.** Casual Friday look

When you are new on a job and you were told to go *Casual Friday*, just take your usual work outfit down a notch until you know what the culture is. When you only heard that they do *Casual Friday*, but you were not invited to participate, just go for your normal work look. Style your outfit in a way that you can easily go down a notch by removing an accessory like a scarf, or necklace when you see how your colleagues are dressed.

To style a *Casual Friday* outfit take a work outfit that fits your *work dress code* and swap one piece for something that is more *casual* or comfortable than the item that it substitutes. However, the outfit still should look professional.

Outfit 1.21. Casual Friday look   **Outfit 1.22**. Casual Friday look

Be aware that the following outfit suggestions may not work in all work places. Take them as inspirations of how to create a *Casual Friday look* rather than coping/recreating them from your own closet. **Outfit 1.19** swaps a *business casual* sweater for a graphic print T-shirt. In **Outfit 1.21**, slacks and a chambray shirt are replaced by boyfriend jeans and a press-button shirt. **Outfits 1.20** and **1.22** replace a regular skirt of a *business casual* work outfit with a denim skirt. Other great *Casual Friday* combinations are:

- Dark wash straight cut jeans instead of slacks, Irish blazer, button-down shirt or fine knit turtleneck sweater, pumps
- Dress pants, oxford shirt uppermost button unbuttoned, small necklace, statement belt/necklace, motorcycle jacket instead of a blazer, pumps
- Chinos, medium wash denim shirt, statement belt/necklace, light fabric summer blazer, pumps
- Denim jacket instead of a blazer, linen summer pants, dressy top

- Cardigan, shirt or blouse, dress pants, pumps
- Printed sheath dress, denim jacket instead of cardigan, pumps

1.6 Office Party

There are corporate and festive office cocktail parties. A general rule is to stay within the broad lines of the *office dress code*'s limits with respect to showing skin in the sense of toes, heels, cleavage, belly, legs, and arms. Keep the rule when the item/look works for date night out, it is not for the office party. Recall the attendees are still your colleagues. Thus, your goal is to look professional even though it is a party.

1.6.1 Festive Office Party

Festive office parties are typically hold during the holiday season. In the creation of an outfit for a festive office party, you can go for sequins, metallic, shine, and embellishments. Even a modest cocktail dress works. A strapless cocktail dress becomes appropriate for a festive office party when worn with a matching bolero, thin fine fabric stole, or a nice leather jacket. However, you have to commit to keeping the cover-up on, no matter how hot the room might be and/or how bad your hot flash might be.

Outfit 1.23. Office party creative field   **Outfit 1.24**. Festive office party

Black slim pants with a metallic, embellished or sequin top are another great option as is a solid top with a sequin or brocade skirt. A holiday dress would also meet the *dress code*. Of course, you are never wrong with a little black dress (LBD). But if you go for one, stay out of the crowd of LBDs by accessorizing with festive rhinestone jewelry or holiday jewelry (belt in **Outfit 1.23**). Go for a big clutch or nice evening bag, i.e. something different than your usual day bag. Embellished stilettos or open toe pumps fit the bill (unless the *office dress code* requires closed shoes).

Stay away from *informal* fabrics, daytime outfits, corporate clothes, suits, or anything denim. Also steer away from anything that is too short or too long (e.g. a maxi dress) and/or shows too much cleavage (back or front, it doesn't matter).

1.6.2 Corporate Office (Cocktail) Party

The corporate office or cocktail party asks more or less for gray or dark *corporate style* as foundation with a twist of color for the blazer and/or the style of the skirt (e.g. a shiny full skirt instead of a pencil or straight skirt; **Outfit 1.24**) or with a twist of the jewelry and/or accessories (**Outfit 1.25**). Recall the office party in the movie "An American President" as an example.

Outfit 1.25. Corporate office party **Outfit 1.26**. Formal office party

Stay away from anything *informal* like knits, jersey, too short or too long, and from too much skin. Cover your arms in agreement with the *office dress code*.

A little black dress (LBD) in a classic cut is always a good idea. However, this also means that many of your colleagues may have the same basic idea. Therefore, a great fit and the choice of the accessories are key to stand out of the crowd. In winter, wearing a silky layering top underneath a sheath dress is acceptable in cold climate regions. Straight skirts with a feminine blouse, or straight slacks in gray or black with a shell and bolero or Chanel-type jacket, or a classic shift dress with patent leather belt and a statement brooch are safe options too. A holiday dress would also meet the *dress code* for a corporate office cocktail party during the holiday season as long as it is not jersey.

To look stylish, use only one statement piece of jewelry, and avoid double blink. In other words, stay on the road of classics with a twist, and avoid to look like a walking Christmas tree. A shiny clutch in silver, gold or neutral color patent leather is perfect. Any bright color other than red is risky. However, the red should be repeated somewhere in the outfit.

Wearing tight is a must. Sheer as well as opaque tights work depending on the climate region. Go for closed toe pumps. Anything less would look too *casual* with tight. In cold climate regions, classic boots will be acceptable on cold winter days with snow outside. Stiletto booties are risky, but may work when they are the only "twist" in the look, i.e. the statement.

Formal office parties or office parties with ball call for *formal* gowns (**Outfit 1.26**) that are in agreement with the *office dress code*.

1.7 Business Travel

Check the forecast issued by the National Weather Service for your destination to wear/pack weather appropriate attire. When there is a risk for showers, pack a folding umbrella. When at the departure location, the weather is fine, store the umbrella in the checked baggage. It reduces the risk of losing it on the plane. Packing an umbrella in the carry-on baggage works as well.

For most of us living in climate regions with cold winters, winter travel to warm regions is a challenge. For an Alaskan, for instance, it means schlepping a down coat around in Florida, Hawaii or Mexico, just because it is 40 below zero upon leaving and/or it might be that cold upon coming back. The best advice to solve this problem is to ask a family member, friend or colleague to bring you to and pick you up at the airport. Slip into the appropriate coat, shoes, etc. for your destination at your home airport and leave the cold weather gear with them. Ask them to bring these items when they pick you up.

Planes are often a little chilly as pilots turn down the ventilation to save fuel. Therefore, bring a light blazer, cardigan or Chilly Jilly to stay comfortable on the plane. A Chilly Jilly in a neutral color can double as a scarf with your coat at the final destination if needed.

Wear shoes that you can easily take off/put on to not annoy everyone in the security line behind you. This means steer away from shoes closed with laces or buckles. Opt for pumps, driving shoes, loafers or moccasins. When your outfit asks for a belt, make sure you have it in your carry-on so you can finish your look once you passed security.

When you have to go from the plane to the meeting make sure to wear wrinkle-free clothes. The outfit must be comfortable when sitting on the plane, but must also meet the *dress code* of the meeting. **Outfits 1.27**, and **1.28** are examples for *business casual* attire that meets these criteria. **Outfit 1.27** also works when slacks are required when you have time to change into winkle free slacks at the airport. **Outfits 1.5**, **1.17** and **1.18** are also suitable for *business travel*. **Outfit 1.28** is an example for work travel in physical science related fields in summer.

Outfit 1.27. Business travel   **Outfit 1.28**. Business travel

When you wear panty hose, make sure you have an extra pair in your purse. During boarding and de-boarding, the risk is high that closures of backpacks, zippers or alike distress your hosiery by accident. Runners never meet the *dress code*.

Here are some work travel outfit suggestions:

- Wool suit, silk sweater, pearls, trench coat, laptop tote, wedge heels, or heeled loafers or medium heel pumps
- Loose shirt dress, pantyhose, cardigan, medium heel pumps, trench coat or blazer
- Shift dress, wool blazer or Chanel-type short jacket, pantyhose,

professional looking coat
- Pants, blazer, light fancy sweater, scarf, pearls, nude sheer socks or socks in the color of the pants/shoes, heeled loafers or medium heel pumps

When the *dress code* is *business casual* try the following:
- Dark straight jeans, silk or cashmere sweater, long statement tassel/pendant necklace or classic pearl necklace, casual blazer, medium high heel pumps or loafers
- White denim jeans, printed top, long statement tassel/pendant necklace or classic pearl necklace, casual blazer, medium high heel pumps or d'Orsay

1.8 Science Conference

Make yourself familiar with the climate of your conference region and the weather forecast. Look at the variability of the climate (minima and maxima of temperature, likelihood of precipitation, etc.). Pack with this knowledge in mind.

Recall, it is always better to be over- than under-dressed. In academia, *business casual* attire is appropriate (**Outfits 1.1, 1.2, 1.11, 1.21, 1.22, 1.27, 1.28**). Thus, you can wear a dark pair of jeans with a button-down shirt, blazer and dress shoes. In warm climates or summer, white denim jeans work too (**Outfits 1.1, 1.2**).

A nice blazer with dark jeans, a knitted silk top, even a high quality graphic T-shirt with scarf or pearl necklace are fine when you are in physical sciences (**Outfit 1.29**). Skirts and dresses are acceptable, but should not be shorter than a hand width above the knees. Italian length, i.e. just hitting your knee cap is best. Skirts ride up when you sit down and you don't want to be remembered for your great legs, but for the great talk you gave. As a general rule, no cleavage for the reason. In physical sciences, people are very liberal, but often look *old-fashioned* when they dress up. Thus, go for classic pieces with a modern twist by using unexpected color combinations, mixing pattern (**Outfit 1.30**) or adding one trendy item.

Remember, the first impression can be nearly as important as your talk. Even if you have already given many talks at conferences, there will always be someone who never saw you before. Thus, treat every conference like it is a job interview (see **Section 1.1**) or like it is the first time you are a speaker.

Avoid large jewelry, and busy prints. If the conference room is large, the likelihood that the speaker will be projected on screens is large too. For this reason avoid hounds tooth, needle-pin prints, or similar small patterns. These type of patterns fail to project well on screens. Instead they can make your audience dizzy. Wear them only when you know the room is small.

When you are on the petite side, i.e. less than 5'4" (1.65 m) in height, wear heels for close to eye contact with your male colleagues. Exercise to walk in your heels so you won't wobble. The practice saves you from looking ridiculous when walking and standing in heels. Never wear brand-new shoes to a conference. After a day of running from one session to another in a large congress building like the Moscone Center in San Francisco, even the blisters on your feet would have blisters.

Outfit 1.29. Conference look

Outfit 1.30. Unmatched suit

Go for a comfortable 2.5 inch (5 cm) heel at conferences. When walking in heels always commit to put your weight onto the ball of your foot. Doing so is easy when you shift your hip stepping forward. Note that wedges are easier to walk and stand in than pumps of same heel height. Thus, wearing wedges may allow for comfort and additional height than 2 inch heel pumps. Consider thick soles (0.5 inch, 1.27 cm or so) if needed.

When giving your talk, "stand like a man" to get respect. This means set your feet slightly apart, shoulders square (I use padded shoulders in my blazer), head up, and stand tight and tall. Don't twill your hair, and no red lips. Go for a natural lip color. The color that most likely flatters you the most is a color that is close to the color of your gums.

Most importantly, make sure you feel confident in your clothes and not like "Judy in disguise." Feeling comfortable comes across as being confident. It is acceptable to have one *signature item* that displays your personality in your professional outfit. In my case, it is a studded cuff.

When you are over 40, ditch the suit. It makes you look *old*. When you are over 40, but look younger than 40, ditch the suit anyway. You don't want to stand in front of a poster that is first authored by your student and coauthored by you and be asked whether your supervisor is at the conference too.

Here is some general advice for everyone who attends a conference:

1. Pack wrinkle free clothes that work for both standing and sitting. Only when the conference is in the Tropics, linen is a good choice as humidity suppresses a bit the wrinkling of linen.

2. Bring at least one outfit more than the conference will last. Someone may spill their drink or meal all over you at the reception, conference dinner or just at the coffee break. Recall scientists are nerdy and fly in a different dimension (most of the time).

3. Go for dark colors as wrinkles are less visible when the items are dark than when they are light.

4. Conference rooms usually are über air-conditioned as conveners overestimate the number of people that will attend their session, especially in times of short funding. Consequently, the rooms are too cold as their thermostats were set with more attendees in mind. Thus, always have a cardigan or blazer handy even when the outside temperatures are way over 80F (26.7°C)

5. Wear your name tag all the time and have safety pins ready to attach the name tag to your clothes. The hanging-around-your-neck name tags tilt, hang at belly-button height, both of which is just awkward when someone, especially male colleagues, actually care about reading your name.

6. Make as many connections as possible. Networking is key. Have your business card ready.

7. Flip flops, Birkenstocks, or sneakers plus shorts and a washed out T-shirt or tank top are never appropriate at a conference, no matter of the season at or climate of the conference location. These items read "I can't wait until I get out of this session to finally enjoy the great outdoors of this awesome conference location."

Outfits 1.29 and **1.30** provide inspirations for conference outfits in physical sciences. Here are further stylish conference outfit suggestions:

- Black straight skirt, printed top, statement belt, white button-down shirt, gray or light blue blazer, printed (non-floral) scarf to add a pop of color, black or gray court-style pumps, large tote in a basic or neutral color

- Steal blue blazer, dark straight jeans, striped button-down shirt, navy, silver or pewter pumps, pearls, large bag for laptop/tablet

- Red blazer, chambray button-down shirt, dark jeans, leopard print pumps, belt with golden buckle, pearl necklace, black large tote

1.9 Awards Banquet, Reception, etc.

Awards banquets and donor receptions ask for *business attire* unless the invitation states a different *dress code*. Depending on the organizer, business attire can mean anything from a three piece suit (e.g. banking, industry, corporate entities) to *business casual* (e.g. universities, sport clubs, engineering firms, consulting firms).

In the first case, a dress suit is a great option with pearls, diamond studs and dress pumps. A skirt or pants suit with a neutral color button-down shirt or oxford and a silk scarf or LBD with pearls, black cour-style pumps and a jacket are safe options too.

Outfit 1.31. Science reception

Outfit 1.32. Authors' reception

In the second case, unmatched suits like a tweed skirt and a blazer with a silk top, and pumps, or a black skirt with a Chanel-type jacket, solid jewel color top, and pumps fit the bill. In winter, a black turtleneck with gray or black wool pants, a hounds-tooth blazer and dress shoes, or a plaid blazer with wool pants, sweater vest, oxford shirt and heeled loafers are acceptable. In physical sciences, even dark jeans with a blazer and high quality T-shirt are acceptable (**Outfit 1.31**). **Outfits 1.1, 1.2, 1.4**, and **1.27** to **1.32** would work in a university setting.

1.10 Fundraising Gala

Fundraising galas are all about being seen for the VIPs of a town. Typically, fundraising galas are *formal* to *semi-formal* events where the gentlemen wear a tuxedo or black three-piece suit and the ladies dress in a full length gown (**Outfits 1.26, 4.11, 4.12**, see **Section 4.4.1** Military Ball) or a cocktail dress unless the *dress code* is announced differently, for instance, as a theme, *business attire* (see **Section 1.6**) or *festive business attire*. In the latter case, sequin tops, brocade blazers, skirts or tops with normal business wear are fine.

1.11 Company BBQ, Picnic or Ice Cream Social

Many   companies organize a BBQ, picnic or ice cream social in summer as a morale booster and for building team spirit. Unless the invitation states a *dress code*, it is best to wear a slightly more *casual* version of the usual office *dress code*. This means that in a corporate work place, even when temperatures are in the 90s and the air is muggy, you should wear closed shoes, hosiery and short sleeves when sandals, sling-backs and open-toe shoes, sleeveless, and bare legs are off limits.

Most of the time these events start an hour prior to the end of business or are held during lunch break. Thus, style your work clothes a bit more *casual* or laid back by untucking a shirt, or tying the shirt tails in a knot instead of tucking them into your skirt. A fine jersey dress instead of a work dress works fine when your work environment is *business casual*. When jeans and a T-shirt are allowed at work or on *Casual Friday*, you can wear Bermuda, or long shorts instead and a T-shirt instead of the jeans.

No matter what the *dress code* is, never wear cutoffs, drop-shoulder, halter tops, strap tops or strapless tops to a work related summer event. For inspirations of BBQ and picnic outfits see also **Sections 2.8** and **2.9**, respectively.

Here some outfit ideas for a *business casual* or *casual* work environment:

- Printed summer dress with cardigan, canvas sneakers (instead of the pumps)
- Boot-cut or straight jeans or white jeans, striped sweater, button-down shirt knotted in front or worn as a jacket, cage sandals with heel
- Printed ¾ sleeve top, full skirt (instead or a straight skirt), wide belt, dress sandals
- Short-sleeve solid bright top, A-line skirt, belt, sandals, statement necklace

2 FAMILY AND FRIENDS

Dressing for success does not stop when it comes to family and friends. Instead it is as important as at work, but with a slight shift of the goal of dressing and purpose.

2.1 Family Reunion

Even when meeting with your family, you have to think about what to wear. Everyone will take photos at a family reunion. The photos will land in a folder. Your photos may be deleted after you are "not" family anymore due to a divorce. This divorce can be yours or the person's, who took the photos. Well, this fate of photos of you is not the one to worry about.

The photos that land on social media when something funny happens to you are not a big deal either. It just happens that someone spills the gravy all over someone else. Everyone feels pity for the poor victim, and finds it funny or tasteless of your family member to post it. Even when nothing funny happens, the photos that are posted during or immediately after the family reunion are not to worry about too.

Photos that are totally fine today may turn into a problem years later after you had worn the *big trend of the year* at a family reunion. The trend everyone wore at that time. The trend that in the aftermath years later seems to be the silliest trend ever. The trend of which in retrospective 20 years later you think "What was I thinking when I bought/wore that outfit?" The photo of an *OOTD* that you are embarrassed to see in a decade or more from now.

You have no intention to be the funny granny/auntie that your (future) grand-kids/nieces and/or nephews giggle about. You never liked being the "babysitter" anyhow. You never liked to be the center of attention and/or the family entertainer to begin with. And who needs the title "fashion victim of the family?"

Wearing today's latest trends at a family reunion puts you at risk to be the amusement of future family reunions when they review photos of past family reunions. The best style advice is to wear something timeless, but true to your style. Recall, for instance, the photos of Jackie O. on the yacht of Aristotle Onassis? She wore a riding jacket, sweater and pants – a timeless *American Classic* look. If Scotti had beamed her into today's streets, it would be hard to identify her by her outfit as being of a different decade.

Let us look at some general, style-type independent aspect of a timeless look. Unless you work in a bar or wear a uniform, anything that was bought with a purpose other than work in mind is risky. You may want to look at the *Casual Friday* or *business Casual* outfits in **Chapter 1** for inspiration of family reunion suitable outfits. Just tune them down with respects to trendy items. This means stay away from neon colors and funny patterns. Also avoid super short skirts or dresses, unusual sleeve styles, sport-team shirts, meant-to-be funny T-shirts, and T-shirts with TV comic figures. They age too. No kid knows Popeye, the Babapapas, or the Pink Panther anymore.

When wearing pants go for a straight cut, which is always in style. Avoid any extremes with respect to your pants. Read no flares, bell-shapes, super wide legs or trendy embellishments or details. For example, the new sexy side-bow-cutout jeans, which shows the skin on the sides of your legs, is cute for the disco now, but not on a family photo in 20 years. Recall you bought it for your vacation trip for going out.

Now let us look into how to put together a timeless outfit in your style. Always pick an outfit that is considered *iconic* for that style. When your style is *Bohemian*, for instance, think of the photos of Ali Mac Graw or Jane Birkin in the 70s. If your style is *Rock 'n Roll*, it will be wise just to go for the red jeans, studded ankle booties, tuxedo shirt, and black motorcycle leather jacket. Leave the trendy skull scarf and the leather jacket with studs and chains all over the place at home. When your style is *California Casual*, look at photos showing Diaz Cameron, Goldie Hawn, Farrah Fawcett, or Joni Mitchell away from the beach for timeless inspiration. In other words, ensure that you tune down the dreamy sexuality, and/or surfer-girl part of this style unless you family reunion is a beach bonfire. In plain English, skip the cutoffs, the spaghetti strap tanks and dresses, the 50 times washed jeans and the Birkenstocks. Instead, wear dark straight or boot-cut jeans, a black top or vertical pinstripe button-down, a white blazer and ballet flats, for instance. Other timeless *California Casual* options are a slouchy knit top with a straight front button skirt, sturdy heel or plateau sandals and a blazer, or dark straight jeans with a slouchy knit top, leather bomber and booties, or boot-cut slightly washed jeans with a dolman sleeved top and strappy sandals.

Outfit 2.1. Classic w. eclectic twist

Outfit 2.2. Classic w. punk twist

Outfit 2.3. Classic w. casual twist

Outfit 2.4. Classic w. Boho twist

Why is it important to stay true to your style and not just wear something *classic* like Michelle Obama during her time as First Lady? You want to feel comfortable in your clothes, which is key to come across as confident, and honest. Sending these messages is especially important when the family reunion is the in-laws part of the family. You want to be regarded as the "best catch" s/he could get, the best that ever happened to your spouse, and as such, as a great addition to the family. Nobody wants to settle for being the "appendix".

When you are not looking forward to family reunions, you are not alone. Many people don't. Keep in mind, it is just a day every so often. Typically, it is even less than a day when you are honest. Make the best out of it. Always remember, the only family members you can choose are your spouse and your pets. The rest are *free bees*. These free bees can be all awesome. Lucky you! Then you have all reasons to look forward to the next family reunion. However, keep in mind, you never know who will join the family in the future. There might be that annoying person, who laughs about everyone but themselves, who will become a future family member. Thus, protect yourself by dressing timelessly at all family reunions. Or like the Godfather said "Keep your friends close, your enemies closer."

Outfit 2.5. Tuned down Rock 'n Roll   **Outfit 2.6**. Classic

The following outfit inspirations also work at family reunions:
- Cashmere sweater, leather pants, layering top, booties, simple necklace
- Classic Irish riding jacket or similar, leather pants, booties, layering top under V-neck sweater, minimal necklace

See also **Sections 3.3** to **3.5** for spring/summer, **3.9** for fall, and **3.10** for further winter family reunion outfit inspirations.

2.2 Bridal Party

June marks the official start of the summer, and in the US also the beginning of wedding season. For us girlfriends, it means to share the extra support for our bride-to-be girlfriends.

The bridal shower is one of the biggest events prior to the wedding. In the US, bridal showers are only attended by the special women in the bride's life. Usually, the maid-of-honor or mother organizes the bridal shower. Occasionally, American bridal showers can be co-mingled especially when held at work. Russian bridal showers are "women only" as they often end up with a striptease of the bride-to-be. German pre-wedding parties are typically attended by the bride and groom together. Everybody who knows about the party can show up. Sometimes these parties may end up with a hunt for the "stolen" bride.

When you are invited to a bridal shower, prepare your outfit depending on the answers to the following questions.

1. Is there a bridal shower theme and/or color? If so, take it as the *dress code*, and follow it.
2. Was there a *dress code* hint on the invitation? If so, follow suit.
3. What is the location of the bridal party? Is it indoors or outdoors, in a bar, at a pool, at work, etc.? Dress with the *dress code* of the location in mind when no *dress code* was given..
4. Is the party *casual*, *semi-formal*, or *formal?* The time and place may provide hints on the *dress code* as well.
5. What is the season, the weather forecast and the actual weather?

The reason to follow the *dress code* (if there is one) is that such coordination yields great photos that are something special for the bride. You don't die wearing a color you don't like for a couple of hours. Just borrow a piece in that color when you would never wear the color again.

Keep in mind that the party is for the bride. Thus, make sure you won't out-dress her. Of course, this advice is hard to follow when you know the bride is on the *frumpy* or *trashy* side. In this case, dim down the glam, but still remain stylish.

In all cases, skirts and dresses are great choices as bridal parties are about being a woman (see also Mother's Day **Section 3.4**), i.e. they have a feminine vibe. Another plus point of skirts or dresses is that they can be styled for any weather (see **Outfits 2.7, 2.8** for a summer and winter suggestion, respectively), and styled up and down with accessories. You can even add the final touch in the restroom at the venue if needed. When you see you are overdressed just take one accessory off to blend in.

Don't sweat the choice of the outfit. The most important points are to celebrate women friendship and share every girl's hope and dream of a "happy ever after." Here are some outfit ideas:

- Tulle skirt, button-down shirt or bold striped sweater, metallic pumps and nude clutch or vice versa
- Blue China print on a white shift dress, nude pumps, cream clutch
- Jewel-tone fit-and-flare dress, nude or metallic clutch, pumps in the pastel shade of the dress
- Pastel lace sheath dress, matching color pumps, cream or metallic clutch
- Floral skirt, matching color solid top, nude or matching color pumps or strappy sandals
- Wide-leg small-print pants, black top, plateau sandals in the background color of the pants, small black fringe shoulder bag
- Little Red Dress with leopard print coat, geometric print bag, black shoes

Outfit 2.7. Bridal shower summer look **Outfit 2.8**. Bridal party look

2.3 Weddings

Many people associate spring with sunshine and hope – a reason why spring is the wedding season in many countries. In Germany, for instance, May is the dream wedding month, because it brings the first real warm days. The vegetation is already green and flowers, bushes and trees are in full bloom – a perfect background scenery on a sunny day.

There are various kinds of *dress codes* for weddings. Typically, the invitation states a *dress code*. If not, let the time be your lead. No matter what the *dress code* is, avoid the following most often made wedding style *faux pas*:

1. Religious jewelry of your own faith when there will be a service of another faith.
2. Skimpy or provocative clothes including corsages and belly-free attire except for saris.
3. Jeans and T-shirts (except for a wedding at a sports club), baseball caps, large view-blocking hats.
4. Casual footwear, sunglasses or bags to your otherwise *semi-formal* outfit.
5. Wearing the color the bridal party, i.e. always find out their color.

Please take the *RSVP* seriously. It means *Respond S'il Vous Plait* (answer please). Even when you don't go, acknowledge the receipt of the invitation and tell the couple that you are unable to come. They don't expect a reason, but your response helps them in the planning of the venue and keeping their costs at bay.

Since weddings are also some sort of family reunion you may want to also read **Section 2.1** prior to making the final decision on your outfit.

2.3.1 Beach Wedding

Being invited to a beach wedding is the most desirable wedding invitation *dress code* wise. Even if you live far away from a beach, you can wear the purchases again and again on your next vacation and on weekends. Moreover, these dresses are much more comfortable than those of other *wedding dress codes* including that you can wear comfortable flat sandals.

Keep the following in mind when shopping for your beach wedding guest outfit:

1. When creating your beach-wedding outfit and you are over 40, resist to go for anything flower-power. The *hippy look* had its time. It was great back then, but it is well past its prime. Today, this look just screams *Old Lady*. It is ridiculous on any woman over 40 unless it was your style all your life. We don't want to re-live our youth again. We love who we are now. Go for a modern *just-right-now* look that is not *over the top*, i.e. avoid extreme trends.
2. Go for a maxi or high-low hem dress that still allows you to wear a bra <u>and</u> shapewear. Even if you will never wear the dress again with a bra and shapewear, at the wedding, you should. Many photos will be taken and you want your "girls" to sit in the right place to not look *frumpy*. You also want your tummy tucked in. Many beach-wedding suitable dresses have cuts that make you look pregnant otherwise.
3. When choosing your dress, be aware that there is always some wind at the beach. A wide skirt caught by the wind might look like

you set the sails. Not to mention that it is hard to walk/stand straight under such conditions.

4. Pick your accessories in the vibe of the dress. Make sure to have one *on-trend* item. More than one is over-kill and to be avoided. It could be the source for laughter for years to come at family reunions (see **Section 2.1**). A straw clutch is a nice option for dresses with a floral or ethnic print. A small cross-body bag looks great on a striped dress.

5. Beach weddings require a pair of comfy thongs, flat mules or strappy sandals with either embellishment, semi-precious stones, Swarovski crystals, or a metallic tone. Since such sandals can be incorporated in your weekend and vacation wardrobe, you can invest some money. These sandals are not like the sky-high heels of a *formal* wedding that you will never wear again. Make sure you break in the thongs, mules or sandals prior to the wedding. Open blisters on a salty beach hurt and would ruin your day. Not to mention that your painful face on the wedding photos would guarantee the amusement of kids at future family parties.

6. When the wedding is during daytime, make sure you get a pair of sunglasses in the vibe of your outfit. When the wedding is in the evening have a stole, wrap, or light jacket that matches the outfit's style to keep you warm after the sun sets over the ocean.

7. Do you recall the photo of the freshly engaged Diana Spencer in a light skirt with a kindergarten kid on her arms that went thru the press for days because of the see-thru? A beach wedding is not the time to show off your legs. You can't control the photographers, but you can take control to avoid being embarrassed. Before buying a dress, check that its fabric is woven tightly enough to avoid see-thru even when you stand with the sun in your back.

Outfits 2.9 and **2.10** show examples of beach wedding outfits. Other great options are:

- Medium-size floral print dress with asymmetric hem, necklace, studs, metallic bag, leopard print flat sandals, sunglasses, straw hat
- Double-layer maxi dress, floral or graphic print scarf, golden sandals, bold short necklace, cross-body mini-bag in a color of the print
- Beaded, sequin-embellished high-low hem floral print dress, metallic flat sandals, cream clutch
- Maxi pink or fuchsia shoulder halter dress with knee-high slit, blue flat sandals, golden clutch, golden tussle necklace, gold color wide bangle with pink and blue stones, golden geometric earrings with blue stones

- Gray high-low hem maxi dress with tussle, coins or feather necklace, matching earrings, small cream tote, tan beaded thongs, straw hat, coin bracelet
- Beaded tank top or silk top, maxi floral wrap skirt, multi bangles in the colors of the print, small straw tote, large 80s style sunglasses, white strappy sandals

Outfit 2.9. Beach wedding, guest   **Outfit 2.10**. Beach wedding, guest

2.3.2 Civil Wedding

The legal part of weddings differs strongly by states and countries. When borough, county, city or religious officers are involved you cannot be wrong with pants or skirt suits, a *formal* dress, anything along the line of *business casual* as long as you leave your jeans at home. What's called *Sunday's Best* like a velvet dress would work too. A cocktail dress with cropped jacket to cover the shoulders during the ceremony may work as long as you are sure not to out-dress the bride.

In some regions, women wear a hat during the official part of the wedding. This accessory makes the outfit very sophisticated. The hardest part is to find a hat that goes with the vibe of the outfit. Furthermore, the brim of the hat should not be too large as you don't want to block the view for the people standing behind you. How lucky are our sisters in Great Britain where there are still hat makers and stores with huge selections.

Here are some outfit inspirations for a formal civil wedding.

- Abstract floral print dress, belt, small lady-like bag, jacket in one of the prints colors, sling-back pumps
- Linen blazer, black straight skirt, polka dot top, silk scarf, pearls, clutch bag, black patent leather pumps
- Black silk or cashmere turtleneck, hounds tooth blazer, pearls, pencil skirt/black pants, black pumps

Outfit 2.11. Civil wedding, guest   **Outfit 2.12**. Civil wedding, guest

2.3.3 Afternoon Wedding

The *dress code* of an afternoon wedding is *semi-formal* which calls for cocktail or party dresses. Fit-and-flare, sheath, high-low hem dresses or retro inspired (read 50s) dresses are great choices. When you like to dance, go for a dress with a pleated or flare to circle skirt. Be sure to wear bikers in a matching color underneath to not show too much leg when you twirl.

When a religious ceremony is involved, avoid strapless and spaghetti straps. When you absolutely want that dress, have a little cover-up like a jacket in a matching fabric and color or the same fabric as your dress, a stole or a fancy coat to wear during the ceremony. In the US, a black pants suit with chiffon top or a tuxedo are great choices too.

Color-wise everything from pastel to gemstone bright colors goes. In the US, find out the color of the bridal party, so you do not choose the same color. Always avoid white unless you are the bride. In many European countries, wearing a LBD or a white dress as guest at a wedding would be considered a tasteless choice. In the US, a LBD is ok, when the vibe of the dress clearly states party. Medium sized (size of your hand) floral print cocktail dresses work well too with metallic pumps or pumps in a color of the print or dress.

Taffeta, tulle, chiffon, lace, jacquard or silk are great fabrics for an afternoon wedding. Stay away from anything too daytime like cotton, jersey, or denim.

Outfit 2.13. Sequin party dress   **Outfit 2.14**. Charcoal lace formal dress

When the party is outside (e.g. garden party, boat party), go for elegant wedge heels that match the vibe of your dress. They help you to walk on a lawn without sinking in and ruining the shoes. Wedges are safer than heels when boarding a boat. Peep toe pumps are great with above-the-knee dresses. When the fabric of the dress is matte, go for patent leather pumps in the same color or black. Nude patent leather works well with gemstone colored dresses. When the dress is shiny, go for suede or velvet pumps. Blush or metallic pumps pair nicely with pastel shade dresses.

Choose a bag in a different color than your shoes, unless you are in your twenties. On us 40+ women, matching bag and shoes looks so *Seventies* and screams *Old Lady*. A metallic clutch with patent leather heels or a patent leather clutch with metallic heels work as well. A sequin clutch with matte open-toe pumps all in adjacent colors on the color wheel or in the same color family are great combinations.

Go for just one statement jewelry piece like a large cocktail ring, large dangling earrings or a statement necklace.

For an outdoor afternoon wedding, check the weather forecast. You may need a cover-up or sunglasses in a matching vibe and color. Aviator with a cocktail dress are a *no-no*.

2.3.4 Formal Wedding

Black Tie weddings have memorable outfits that address the formality of the event. In the US and the Common Wealth, be aware that the style of wedding-guest dresses differs from that of the mother-of-the-bride/groom and the bridesmaid dresses. Make sure you shop for/rent a special occasion dress when you are a guest, and pick a mother-of-the-bride/groom dress when this is your role at the party. In both cases, stay out of the territory of bridesmaid dresses, and of course avoid white and the color of the bridal party.

Outfit 2.15. Red formal dress   **Outfit 2.16**. Blue formal gown

A *black tie* wedding is not just dark organza one shoulder dresses with pearl clutch and d'Orsay pumps. There are great dresses that have boat necks and cover the arms (e.g. **Outfit 2.15**). A full skirt organza tea-length dress with crew neck and long sleeves is a great option for petites. These kind of dresses look great with glittery stilettos and a sleek top knot. A chiffon strapless or asymmetric strap special occasion dress (**Outfit 2.16**) makes an entrance when paired with a miniature metal clutch, and silver sandals. However, make sure you have the right bra as there is nothing as unflattering than a shoulder-free strapless dress when your girls sit at a different height then the mid of your upper arm.

2.4 Graduation

When you are the graduate, it is straight forward what to wear. The same is true when you are the faculty (**Outfit 2.17**). But what to wear when you are the mother of the graduate?

Outfit 2.17. Doctoral gown   **Outfit 2.18**. Graduation guest

Well of course not, what Mrs. Robinson was wearing in "The Graduate." Instead, create an outfit that is comfortable for sitting thru three hours, and can go from the early morning festivities to the reception after commencement. When the commencement is in a station, make sure you have sunglasses and some cover-up like a cardigan or jacket that matches your outfit. Indoor multi-purpose halls may be air-conditioned and chilly. Having a warp, shawl or wide scarf is a good backup plan for both venues. Go for light colors (**Outfit 2.18**) and steer away from black. A medium-size lady-like tote or messenger bag is practical to carry a cover-up, your camera, a bottle of water, sun screen, reading glasses and a book. Other great outfit options for graduation guests are:

- Sundress, statement belt, summery clutch or small tote bag, kitten heel or wedge sandals
- Pencil skirt, button-down shirt, 2.5 inch (7.5 cm) classic pumps, cardigan, lady-like bag

- Midi chiffon dress, strappy sandals, day clutch, cropped jacket
- Silky joggers, white button-up shirt, long leopard print or striped jacket, small shoulder bag, open-toe pumps

2.5 Movies

Going to the movies is a great way to escape reality for two hours. Who doesn't love that? But going there requires a reality check on what to wear. The challenges are on several burners. First, in an only partly filled theater AC can be so strong that even someone used to subarctic conditions ends up feeling uncomfortable. Another aspect to think about is your company and your plans after you come out of the cinema or before heading there. Depending on the answers to the following questions your outfit should be *dressy* or *casual*.

1. Are you going with your significant other, the girls, friends, kids or teenagers?
2. Will you go out for dinner or a drink before/afterwards or stir home?

2.5.1 Dressy at the Movies

Movie night with your significant other or the girlfriends calls for dressing up. Go dressier for your significant other (**Outfit 2.19**) than with the girls. Lean more to *dressy casual* (**Outfit 2.20**) when you are going with friends. Keep in mind what the significant other or your friends might wear to not look out of place.

A printed dress with cardigan or a loose skirt with top and cardigan are *casual*, but feminine and *dressy*, and still work for a drink after the movies as well. The cardigan protects from chilly AC or nighttime radiative cooling later in the evening. It can be knotted around the shoulders or hips when it is too warm to wear the cardigan. This look is moreover really stylish.

Accessorize with a matching necklace and studs or long earrings with bangles/bracelets. Flats or canvas sneakers look cute with a printed or solid fit-and-flare dress (**Outfit 2.19**) and are great for a walk to the restaurant or bar in warm climate regions and/or in summer. Low heel sandals, loafers, or booties are great options too when you can walk in heels. When you live in a cold climate region, and/or during the cold season, wear tights in a matching color to the dress/skirt or shoes to elongate your legs. Add a saddle, bucket, hobo or any type of bag that does not read office, sport, travel or evening bag to finish the look.

Here are additional *dressy* outfit suggestions:
- Statement skirt while keeping everything else *casual* makes a (risky, but fun) movie outfit
- Leather baseball jacket, denim skirt, T-strap pumps, Chanel-type bag, striped T-shirt, tussle necklace (**Outfit 2.20**)

- Print dress, cardigan, cross-body mini bag, pumps
- Fit-and-flare dress with feminine detail like a bow or embroidery, booties, matching tight, cardigan
- Silver or gold foil pleated skirt, chambray shirt, denim jacket, black bag, kitten heels

Outfit 2.19. Dressy look   **Outfit 2.20**. Dressy casual look

2.5.2 Casual at the Movies

While the above outfit suggestions are easy to dress down towards more *casual*, skirts or dresses are often unpractical when you have to watch kids at the movies. Cleaning a dress or skirt often means a trip to the dry cleaner.

When you have kids in your party, go for jeans with a nice top or T-shirt plus a cardigan/jacket. Accessorize with an infinity scarf or knot your scarf to reduce the risk to lose it when running after kids prior/after the movie or during the break between the advertisements and the film. **Outfit 2.21** is a variation of this outfit idea with cargos and utility jacket, while **Outfit 2.22** is a winter version.

Think twice when deciding on your jewelry. Necklaces could be ripped by toddlers. Leave your arm party at home. You will have to reach for the kids several times during the movie when they get frightened/excited. Thus, bangles would be too noisy.

Desert boots, canvas sneaker or booties allow you to move fast. Only when you can catch a bus running in heels, heels are fine. Go for a shoulder or even better a cross-body bag to keep your hands free. The following outfits serve you well when you take kids to the movies:

- Long-sleeved T-shirt, cardigan, scarf, boyfriend jeans, statement belt, ballet flats, saddle bag
- Oversize cable-knit sweater, layering top, shoulder or cross-body bag, straight or stretch skinny jeans, booties

Outfit 2.21. Casual with camo   **Outfit 2.22**. Casual look

2.6 Dinner Party

Dinner parties – whether at a friend's or colleague's house or in a restaurant – are those in between *dress-up* and *casual* social events that are hard to dress for. While the *dress code* for a cocktail party (see **Sections 1.6.2, 3.11.1**) and a BBQ (**Section 2.8**) are straight forward *dress-up* and *casual*, respectively, the *dinner-party dress code* seems to be quite vague to many of us. Here are some aspects to consider in striking the balance to feel comfortable, appropriately dressed for the event, respectful, and to have a great time.

First make sure whether the hostess/host has planned a *theme*. If so, you will be out of the salad. You just have to find something that matches the theme or at least shows your intend to go with the theme. When there isn't a theme, your goal should be to wear something *fashionable*, but not too trendy. *Trendy* is for girls' night out.

Avoid showing up in a full-on outfit of one designer or high-end clothes like a Chanel jacket. Spilling of wine and gravy just happen at dinner parties (see **Sections 2.1**, **3.9.3**, **3.10**). On the other side, don't dress *casual* as a dinner party is more fancy than a BBQ (**Section 2.8**). You outfit also should not read *work outfit*. Note that when you are an immigrant in America, the easiest dinner outfit is to wear clothes of your heritage (e.g. **Outfits 3.13**, **3.14**). Be aware that regional differences within your original country are beyond the radar. If you were born in Germany, for instance, a dirndl will do. When you were born in India go for a sari. You get the idea. Everyday heritage clothing may be a great ice breaker at a dinner party. In the European Alps or Scandinavia, wearing a cotton or wool dirndl is always appropriate for a dinner party. Stay away from linen as it easily wrinkles when sitting at the table.

Outfit 2.23. Dinner party look

Outfit 2.24. Dinner party look

Dinner parties are your "Card Blanche" to accessorize with cocktail rings, chunky necklaces (**Outfit 2.23**), layer necklaces, or don an oversize scarf, but please only one of these accessories at a time. Dinner parties are a good opportunity to wear that shrunken blazer, embellished cardigan, or flowy dress. Unusual colors (**Outfit 2.24**), patterns or cuts also fit the bill. In warm climate and/or summer, go for slouchy silky pants or tops, but make sure to have only one slouchy item per outfit. In colder climate regions and/or winter, silk and/or cashmere knit tops and heavy fabrics like jersey, gabardine or even white denim are in order.

The type of shoes should be picked with the vibe of your outfit in mind. Nearly everything not too *casual* and not too *fancy* works, for instance, wedges, strappy or beaded sandals with no to a little heel, cut-out ballet flats, even booties when they fit to the vibe of the other items.

Switch your bag. The bag should clearly be outside the territory of *black tie* or *work*. Go for a not too large clutch or other fancy bag that meets the vibe of the outfit. If you live in a cold climate region where it is expected that you take off your boots in winter, you may consider bringing house slippers, non-slip socks, flatouts or other indoor shoes. Pick the shoes you plan to wear inside with your outfit in mind. Don't wear Marlene Dietrich style pants or flare jeans that call for plateau soles or other long pants that require heels to not step into/onto the hem when it is the first time you are invited there. You can only wear these types of pants when you know that you will not have to take off your shoes! Pants cut for plateau shoes or shoes with heels become a hazard without them. The same applies to maxi dresses or skirts (**Outfit 2.25**).When you bring your shoes, put them in a big bag (**Outfit 2.23**), statement color tote or printed fabric bag.

Outfit 2.25. Dinner party at a roadhouse **Outfit 2.26**. Dinner party LBD

Avoid anything too *festive* or *glam*, especially when the party is at a home, not a restaurant. You do not want to out-dress your hostess who runs back and forth between the kitchen and the dining table! Unless she has a maid who prepares and serves the dinner, she will not wear something too *fancy* due to the risk of spilling and ruining it. When the dinner party is at a restaurant, keep the (unwritten) *dress code* of that place in mind when putting together your outfit. In an Alaska roadhouse, for instance, anything chiffon would be out of place in winter. Here are some dinner outfits that work well:

- Printed dress, ballet flats, belt, whimsical necklace
- Tweed skirt, floral top, belt, embellished flats
- Culottes or wide pants (when they are in fashion), fancy top, long pendant necklace, kitten heel pumps
- Fit-and-flare dress, ballet flats, pearl necklace.
- Floral cardigan, tank top, statement belt, white jeans, strappy sandals, small bag
- Printed dress, cardigan, pointy toe flats, scarf, mini bag, earrings
- Fit-and-flare dress, cardigan, tight, booties, small shoulder bag
- Flowy lace dress, denim jacket, open toe booties or ankle high sandals, statement belt
- Plaid shirt, denim jacket, Hosentürle skirt, flat sandals (**Outfit 3.12**)
- Midi or tea-length chiffon or lace dress, motorcycle vest or jacket or denim jacket
- LBD dressed down with casual shirt and tight (**Outfit 2.26**)

Finally, two other things. Bring a little thoughtful gift for the host/hostess. Whatever you wear make sure it will not make you feel uncomfortable when you are "forced" to over-eat (see **Section 3.9** Thanksgiving).

2.7 Sunday Brunch

Going out for brunch – a mix of breakfast and lunch – is very common in America. Many Americans leave their house for church without breakfast and head over to a restaurant afterwards. Thus, the *dress code* for brunch is *modest* in all places. However, it may vary strongly with respect to formality depending on the religious background, i.e. the crowd that typically goes to a given brunch place and the (unwritten) *dress code* of the restaurant. Places frequented by customers mainly from academia are on the most *casual*, while places with high percentage of military customers are on the more *dressed up* end of the spectrum.

Keep jewelry at minimum, i.e. steer away from arm parties, charm bracelets, layering of necklaces or chandelier earrings. They are too noisy to follow the conversation with your party. Long necklaces may end up in your plate when you walk from the buffet to your seat.

When choosing your outfit and not knowing the kind of guests, keep in mind that it is always better to be over-dressed than under-dressed. It is a good idea to err on the *modest* and *conservative* side (see also **Section 3.3** Easter Brunch). Avoid anything lacy, sheer, sleeveless, too much cleavage, too short, or too *casual*. Here are some suggestions:

- Straight or A-line midi skirt, small print floral, pin stripes or polka dot shirt or top, fine knit cardigan, small handle day bag, court shoes
- Pencil or straight skirt, (faux) twinset, necklace, small fold-over shoulder bag, moccasins or kitten heel pumps
- Straight dress or sheath with sleeves, short jacket or coat, sturdy heel pumps, small day bag
- Dark jeans, white shirt, blazer, pointy or round toe pumps

Outfit 2.27. Brunch winter look   **Outfit 2.28**. Brunch winter look

2.8 BBQ

For many American families, Memorial Day is the official start of summer and the BBQ season. At a BBQ, food, drink, and grass spots are possible. Thus, avoid any sensitive fabrics or clothes that need to be dry cleaned. Nevertheless, you want to create a cute, subtly *fashion-forward* outfit. Statement earrings or a statement necklace are great to add a *trendy* item.

When the BBQ is in the afternoon, a hat and sunglasses are must-haves and should be part of your look. Let your outfit be the guide whether to go for a floppy sunhat, a baseball cap, or a straw fedora. The same applies for the style of your sunglasses. Aviators don't look great with a *Bohemian* maxi dress, while cat eyes or round glasses do.

Denim and khaki pants or shorts with a cute T-shirt or cotton top are a no-brainer. Linen drawstring pants are a nice alternative to khakis and jeans.

Pair these options with a straw fedora or baseball cap. Don't turn your baseball cap backwards when you are over 40. It is not fun at our age. A cotton maxi dress or crochet dress are other light-weight option. When you go for a dress, go for a floppy hat. Make sure that a *Bohemian* look stays modern and does not like trying to re-live the 70s.

When the BBQ is in the evening hours, have a cardigan, utility or denim jacket handy. When you are wearing a dress, a stole is a great stylish cover-up when it chills down after sunset. A cardigan over the dress is an *American Classic*. The choice of your cover-up should match the vibe of your outfit.

Your shoes have to be save on unpaved ground when the BBQ is outside. On a lawn or dirt, moccasins, clogs, espadrilles, ballet flats, embellished flip-flops, *old-school* canvas sneakers, gladiators (**Outfit 2.29**), thongs (**Outfit 2.30**) or flat sandals are your best options. Like for outdoor weddings (see **Section 2.3.3**), stay away from plateau sandals to avoid injury.

Outfit 2.29. Casual chic BBQ look   **Outfit 2.30**. BBQ casual look

Think of your shoes also as an accessory that has to match the vibe of your outfit. Clogs, embellished sandals or flip-flops look great with a *Bohemian* maxi dress. Moccasins look great with linen drawstring pants or cutoffs. Canvas sneakers look awesome with full skirt, fit-and-flare and shirt dresses – think Taylor Swift in the Keds ads.

When the BBQ is in a park, go for a cross-body bag to have your hands free to handle the plate. A bag that stands on its own may work when the

BBQ is in someone's yard and you know that it is safe standing at the wardrobe. When you use a bucket bag, tote or basket at a BBQ in public, make sure that someone of your family and/or friends stays at the table when you head to the grill for a first or second.

When attending a BBQ try one of the following outfit suggestions:

- Shorts, gingham button-down shirt or striped T-shirt with scarf, statement belt, straw cap, sandals (**Outfit 2.30**)
- Boyfriend jeans, espadrilles, sweater, utility jacket, sunglasses, shoulder bucket bag
- Blue and white striped midi dress with front button closure, white cardigan, statement belt, straw bag, tan flat sandals
- White shirt dress, floppy straw hat, bright color flat sandals, flats or canvas sneakers
- Floral dress, floppy straw hat, metallic thongs or sandals, cross-body mini bag
- Boyfriend jeans, utility jacket, sweater, espadrilles, aviator sunglasses, small saddle bag

2.9 Picnic

Since at a picnic, you are munching on all kind of stuff that might drip onto your clothes, go for an outfit in fabrics that are low maintenance with respect to cleaning. The fabric should be breathable to not soak in sweat. Wrinkle-free cotton is a nice option.

The style of your outfit can be a *romantic* (**Outfit 2.31**), floral, *Bohemian* (**Outfit 2.32**) or a *countryside* inspired dress or skirt with top. Jeans or a wide or A-line denim skirt with a button-down plaid shirt or T-shirt are great options as well. Other great options are Bermuda shorts or capris with a *girly* or floral top and ballet flats. Or go the *Euro Chic* way and style them with a cap sleeve knit-top or a 3/4 sleeve striped top and ballet flats like Brigit Bardot.

Hot summer heat often leads to swollen feet. Flip flops, thongs, mules (**Outfit 2.32**), slides, the *trendy* orthopedic sandals of the year or woven leather sandals are great footwear for a picnic. When you go for orthopedic sandals, opt for metallic or patent leather and an outfit where they are a natural match without looking *frumpy* or *sloppy*. Leather sandals, embellished thongs or clogs look great with the dress and skirt as well as jeans outfits. All these footwear options are easy to flip off when you sit down on a blanket or folding chair.

On hot, muggy summer days, convective clouds may quickly turn into thunderstorms with gust fronts. Be prepared with a wind breaker or at least a cardigan for layering. After the storm, the air cools down due to evaporative cooling and cold downdrafts.

The style of your outfit can be a *romantic* (**Outfit 2.31**), floral, *Bohemian* (**Outfit 2.32**) or a *countryside* inspired dress or skirt with top. Jeans or a wide or A-line denim skirt with a button-down plaid shirt or T-shirt are great options as well. Other great options are Bermuda shorts or capris with a *girly* or floral top and ballet flats. Or go the *Euro Chic* way and style them with a cap sleeve knit-top or a 3/4 sleeve striped top and ballet flats like Brigit Bardot.

Hot summer heat often leads to swollen feet. Flip flops, thongs, mules (**Outfit 2.32**), slides, the *trendy* orthopedic sandals of the year or woven leather sandals are great footwear for a picnic. When you go for orthopedic sandals, opt for metallic or patent leather and an outfit where they are a natural match without looking *frumpy* or *sloppy*. Leather sandals, embellished thongs or clogs look great with the dress and skirt as well as jeans outfits. All these footwear options are easy to flip off when you sit down on a blanket or folding chair.

On hot, muggy summer days, convective clouds may quickly turn into thunderstorms with gust fronts. Be prepared with a wind breaker or at least a cardigan for layering. After the storm, the air cools down due to evaporative cooling and cold downdrafts.

Outfit 2.31. Picnic outfit

Outfit 2.32. Picnic outfit

When dressing for a picnic, keep potential hazards of the picnic place in mind. In Europe, most picnics are on blankets, meaning grass spots alert! In the US, most picnics involve deck chairs or wooden table-and-bench sets.

The advantage of deck chairs is that you can wear something *fancy* like a clean bias-cut, a white dress or a 40s inspired tea-dress. Their big disadvantage is that embellishments and crochet dresses, jackets or tops can get stacked on the metal and end up ripped. Wood benches at a picnic place bear the same risk. At a picnic in Alaska, have a can of pepper spray handy or someone who runs slower than you.

Great bag options for a picnic besides a basket are a straw bag or fabric satchel. The bag should be large enough to hold sunglasses, wipes, sun screen, mosquito repellant, band aids, a tide stick in case of spills, pepper spray, cardigan or stole and a rain jacket.

2.10 Vacation
2.10.1 Travel

When you travel from a cold place to a warm place in winter, leave your coats in the trunk of your car in the parking garage when it is heated. It is too much hassle at a warm destination to carry a down coat around upon arriving when you have to handle the baggage, keep an eye on the kids while searching for the shuttle, bus, or while renting a car. When your home airport only has an outside parking lot or an open parking deck, leaving outerwear in the trunk is not a good idea. The pieces will be frigid cold when you come back and want to wear them. To outsmart this recipe for catching a cold, ask a friend for a ride and to take/bring the outerwear with them when dropping you off/picking you up.

Since planes are often chilly, bring a blanket scarf (see **Section 1.7** Business Travel). You can use it later at the beach or pool. A light jacket, cardigan or a cotton sweater over a T-shirt are other options.

Wear shoes without laces or buckles that are easy to take off/put on when going thru security. Flip flops are for the beach and pool, not the airport. They belong in the baggage, not on your feet while on travel. They just look cheap, and are a hassle to run in when you try to catch a connection. Furthermore, they break every stylish outfit except *surfer beach style*. Leave the heels for the female CEOs and managers in First Class, unless you are a ballroom dancer or you walk on heels since seventh grade.

Since you have to sit on the plane for a long time, wear clothes that resist wrinkling. When you wear jeans, go for a loose cut or a jeans with stretch (**Outfit 2.33**). A waistband cutting into your belly is uncomfortable. Steer away from sweat pants, they have their name for a reason, and belong into the gym (**Section 2.12**). When your outfit asks for a belt or jewelry as finishing touches, put these items in your carry-on and finish your look once you passed security.

Here are five comfy, but *effortlessly stylish* travel outfit ideas for vacation travel or travel to visit family and friends:

- Long-sleeve tunic, long sweater or trench coat, long T-shirt underneath the trench (you may have to take the trench coat off at security), leggings, ballet flats or pointy toe flats

- Loose jersey dress, cardigan, ballet/pointy toe flats or *old school* fabric sneakers
- Boyfriend jeans, sleek striped long sleeve T-shirt, printed wide scarf (double-duty as blanket), ballet or pointy toe flats
- Jeggings, long slouchy white T-shirt, long black cable-knit or grandpa knit-collar cardigan, light or open toe booties
- Loose printed skirt, ballet flats, striped or solid T-shirt, cropped denim jacket or cardigan

Outfit 2.33. Casual travel outfit   **Outfit 2.34**. Casual travel look

2.10.2 Sightseeing

Since sightseeing involves being inside and outside, check the weather forecast of the local National Weather Service office to be prepared for the weathers. For rain, have a light-weight rain jacket or trench coat handy. You can check the wet jacket or coat with the coat clerk when visiting a gallery/museum. A pocket umbrella is an alternative, but will be difficult when you need both hands for pulling maps on your cell phone. When it is windy a rain coat, rain jacket or trench coat are better than an umbrella. Wind re-directs rain to have an angle versus the vertical. Consequently, rain will reach your lower body despite of carrying an umbrella. Wet clothes are often the reason for catching a cold. On sunny days, make sure to put on sun screen as directed and wear sunglasses.

Sightseeing in metropolitan areas typically includes being on public transportation and on your feet a lot. Comfortable shoes that you can walk in are key. Of course, you can rely on your running shoes. However, water proof sneakers or walking shoes are much more *stylish* options. In summer, comfortable sandals may be a good choice too when the weather is dry and you wear a skirt or dress. Most skirts don't look great with walking shoes.

Visiting museums and galleries means air conditioning, while it may be hot outside. Thus, go for a shirt/top plus sweater, cardigan (**Outfit 2.35**) or *casual* jacket combination. When being outside, you can knot the cardigan, sweater or jacket around your waist or shoulders, which always looks *stylish*. You wear it inside to stay comfortable in the chill of the AC.

Outfit 2.35. Casual sightseeing look   **Outfit 2.36**. Classic sightseeing look

Safe sightseeing outfits are jeans or chinos with a T-shirt, button-down shirt or sweater depending on the temperatures. Opt for a loose/relaxed cut with your jeans or chinos. It is just so much easier to walk up the stairs in the tower of Cologne Cathedral or in St. Paul's Cathedral in a relaxed cut than in skinny jeans.

By all means stay away from rucksacks. You risk to throw something down when turning around in a museum/gallery. Backpacks are also an annoyance when you use public transportation. You may hit kids in the face with your backpack. Not to mention that a backpack identifies you as a tourist and increases your risk of becoming a victim of theft.

Go for a cross-body bag instead. It is *stylish* and leaves both hands free for checking google maps and directions on your cell phone, holding a catalog, taking pictures, carrying your latte or ice-cream cone, handling the metro ticketing machine or holding on to a handrail on the train.

Add a nice necklace or scarf for style. When you are worried about getting your wallet and passport stolen, wear one of the infinity scarfs with sewn-in pockets. They are less obvious than belt bags. Furthermore, the latter make you look pregnant when you close your rain coat during a shower. Here are further outfit inspirations for sightseeing:

- Boyfriend jeans, utility jacket, sweater, espadrilles, aviator sunglasses, cross-body leather bag
- Light summer pants, statement belt, chambray shirt, trench coat, shoulder tote, dress sneakers, pearl necklace
- Capris, solid or floral top, leopard print or striped cardigan, shoulder strap bag, ballet flats or moccasins (**Outfit 2.36**)
- Striped T-shirt with trench coat, boyfriend jeans, shoulder bag, rain boots
- Lace-up walking shoes or boots, above-the-knee denim skirt, statement belt, graphic T-shirt, scarf, raincoat

2.10.3 Resort Style

A great thing about a summer vacation at a resort is that summer resort dresses are relatively cheap, especially when you buy timeless and better quality pieces on sale after the season, or a timeless *retro style* version that you accessorize with *contemporary* pieces for a sophisticated modern look. Of course, always go for the highest quality you can afford.

Always make sure that you can wear a bra underneath when you want to. Solid color resort dresses can easily change their vibe when you style them with different accessories. A statement leather belt takes a resort dress up a notch (**Outfits 2.37, 2.38**). Invest in a little white dress (LWD) as they can be styled easily up and down.

Mix inexpensive with more expensive items for great style. When you go for a resort dress in a cheap fabric, up your look with higher quality accessories than the dress to achieve *ageless style*. Adding cheap accessories to a cheap resort dress make the entire outfit look *trashy*, which is not the style you want ever.

Resort dresses look great with metallic, embellished or simple leather thongs. Espadrilles are another great option. Flat gladiators in tan look great with ethnic print, stripe or chevron dresses. For petites canvas sneakers are cute too when the hem is around the knee and the dress has a floral or polka dot print.

Maxi dresses should not sweep the floor, but end just above the feet.

Stir away from a dress with front slit, as a front slip looks awkward when you sit at the bar. High-low or handkerchief hems (**Outfit 2.37**) are great to show off your legs. A large silk scarf or shear cotton scarf make great cover-ups when it gets chilly in the evening. As always, show skin strategically. Keep in mind, less skin is more *stylish*. Furthermore, coverage protects your skin from aging.

Outfit 2.37. Handkerchief resort dress   **Outfit 2.38**. Resort LWD

Cross-body mini-bags in the vibe of the dress are great for an afternoon stroll and lunch. Have a straw beads-embellished, embroidered or fabric clutch for dinner. Stay away from *glam* clutches.

Wood necklaces, bangles and wood watches are great accessories. Necklaces with colored beads look great with marine striped or solid resort dresses. Go either for long earrings or sunglasses when wearing your hair down and a hat (**Outfit 2.38**). All four in one outfit are overload.

2.11 Spa

When you and your girlfriends haven't been at the selected spa before, check their web site for their *dress code*. When there is nothing mentioned, ask whether they have a *dress code*, when you call to make the reservation. You may also ask whether they provide robes and towels.

On your way to the spa, wear a comfortable and practical outfit like neat yoga bottoms, or lounge pants with a T-shirt, sweater or hoodie. Some guests show up in gym wear and sneakers and a jacket (**Outfit 2.39**). Tie your hair back or up. Arrive without makeup to the spa so treatment can start immediately.

Outfit 2.39. Going to the spa look   **Outfit 2.40**. Gym wear

At a spa, you spend a lot of time in your robe. When you got often invest in a practical robe in your style. An awesome spa outfit adds to feeling great and increases the relax factor.

Flip-flops and slides are great footwear options. When they also have exercising equipment bring clean sneakers in case you want to use it.

2.12 Gym

Gym wear should allow freedom of motion and be breathable to avoid overheating. It should be tight enough to not be caught in equipment. Cotton leggings with some spandex for shape in a cute print or solid and graphic print T-shirts look neat (**Outfit 2.40**). For aerial yoga, get a bra top. A T-shirt would expose of your sport bra when you hang upside down. Ask your personnel trainer or coach which footwear they recommend for your workout.

3 HOLIDAYS

3.1 Valentine's Day

The big question on Valentine's Day is what to wear. As so often in life, no one hard answer exists. What to wear depends on a couple of factors. Take the answers to the following questions into account when choosing the outfit for the big night out.

1. Where will we go?
2. How long do you know each other?
3. How will we get there?
4. What is in the weather forecast?

Going to the movies, for instance, is a casual Valentine's Day date calling for a *dressy casual* look. Your goal should be to put together an outfit that highlights your best feature or shows your shape in an understated way (**Outfit 3.1**). For instance, skinny jeans, a wrapped top, motorcycle booties, and a slouchy cardigan are a great choice. An *American Classic* outfit is a cardigan over a cute belted floral print dress that just shows your collar bone and ends above the knees. See also **Section 2.5** Movies.

Going to a restaurant means you can dress up. Keep the *dress code* of the restaurant in mind when picking the outfit. You can never go wrong with a LBD with the right accessories. On Valentine's Day, one can say the same for the little red dress (LRD, **Outfit 3.2**). See also **Section 2.6** Dinner Party.

When you go to a Valentine's ball or dance party check the *dress code*. When it is *formal*, go for a gown not shorter than knee-length (see also **Section 4.4** Dance Events). When it says *semi-formal*, a long gown could be over-kill. Go for a cocktail dress or party dress instead (e.g. **Outfit 2.13**). To a social dance, a *fancy* fit-and-flare dress with some red will do the trick (e.g. **Outfit 2.18**). An *informal* or *casual dress code* permits metallic pants or a sequin skirt with a cute top. Jeans with an embellished or sequin top are great casual choices as well. For any dance, you should have shoes with leather sole or dance shoes. The suede soles of dance shoes and leather soles permit easy twisting and turning. Consequently, it is less likely that your knees and ankles hurt on the next day than when you dance with rubber soles.

When you just started dating or it is your first date, go for more coverage than when you know each other already for a long time. A knee-long long-sleeve fitted crewneck LBD or LRD with tight is perfect. It show-casts your body without looking over the top sexy. You don't want him to stare at whatever. You want him to look into your eyes and talk with you so you get to know each other better.

Outfit 3.1. Valentine at a road house   **Outfit 3.2**. Valentine's Day LRD

If you know each other for quite a while, you can show more skin. But one area at a time is so much more sexy and attractive than skin everywhere. In other words, show skin strategically. Either wear a mini skirt not shorter than 3 to 4 inch (7.5 to 10 cm) above the knee or show cleavage or shoulders, not all at once. Recall, you are celebrating your relationship.

If you have private transportation, you can wear hot high heel sandals or pumps even in cold climate regions. However, when you have to walk and/or wait for public transportation, a pair of shoes that provides good insulation from the ground, but allows to walk safely even on snow and/or ice is your best choice. Typically, shoes with profile soles perform better on ice and/or snow than plain or leather soles. Thus, you should not wear your dance shoes outside.

When the weather requires a coat, pick the coat with your outfit in mind. For instance, avoid wearing a light colored shearling coat over a LBD or velvet dress. You dress may look like you slept in a dog kennel when you take the coat off. When you wear an evening gown, go for a faux fur jacket. When your indoor outfit is made of thin, delicate fabric, have a light cashmere cardigan that you add for extra insulation under the coat at below freezing temperatures. Pick a cardigan that looks great with your indoor outfit as you may need it as a cover-up in a chilly restaurant.

3.2 St. Patrick's Day

Despite St. Patrick was born in Britain, the traditions of celebrating St. Patrick's Day came back to Ireland over the pond as a great spring tourism marketing opportunity. On St. Patrick's Day, Irish-American communities celebrate with parades and parties.

Unless you go to a parade, party or celebrate St. Patrick's Day there is no need to wear green on March 17. However, when you want to fit in the spirit of the day, don't overdo it. A head-to-toe meadow green monochromatic outfit never looks great, not even on St. Patrick's Day. It is plain ridiculous at any age, unless it's a sport uniform or you are Kermit the frog. Therefore, wear just one green items and/or hints of green (**Outfit 3.3**).

Outfit 3.3. Plaid shirt w. green sweater   **Outfit 3.4**. Irish blazer

A fun way is to keep people guessing whether your pop of green is because of St. Patrick's Day or not. You can achieve this by wearing a plaid shirt (**Outfit 3.3**), scarf, or striped sweater with green in the pattern. When meadow green is not in your color palette, go with another green shade like lime green, hunter green, olive (**Outfit 2.27**), chartreuse (**Outfit 2.24**), or teal to demonstrate the intend. You can also opt to just sport some Irish spirit by wearing an Irish blazer (**Outfit 3.4**) or cable-knit sweater (**Outfit 2.25**). Here are further outfit ideas for St. Patrick's Day:

- Green dress, color-blog or nude pumps, pearl necklace
- Hounds-tooth sheath dress, Irish green turtleneck, knee-high boots
- Irish green turtleneck sweater, white pants, white or nude pumps, pendant necklace
- Irish cable knit sweater, jeans, booties
- Irish blazer with jeans/slacks, button-down shirt, pumps or oxfords

3.3 Easter Brunch

Going out for Easter Brunch is all about *dress-up*. No matter how cold it is still outside, ditching the tight and boots and going bare legs in sandals or pumps is a must for many American women of all ages. The new spring dress gets its first appearance. In climate regions with cold winters, boyfriends and husbands alike drop the female part of their party at the door of the brunch place because it is impossible to walk in heels on leftover snow and/or thru a muddy dirt parking lot. Furthermore, it is still way too cold for their ladies' outfits.

Actually, from a health point of view, the tradition to define Easter as the onset of spring fashion is *old-fashioned*. Instead, you should dress with the weather in mind. On Easter, however, any cold gear is *so yesterday* in the US. The Easter Brunch queue at the buffet is the catwalk for the new spring outfits.

To dress for Easter Brunch is a challenge. On one hand side, it is a family and religious event, on the other hand, a brunch and social event (see **Section 2.1** Family Reunion, **Section 2.7** Sunday Brunch). Many pictures will be taken. Thus, last year's dress won't do the trick. Many family members most likely see you only so often. They will remember last year's dress. The outfit should not to be too *trendy* either as it should not cause a major laugh attack of future kids in the family when they look at the photos in ten, twenty, or thirty years.

Go for a *classic* spring skirt-top combination or dress with floral or other timeless prints and a *modest*, read office-appropriate, neckline. Add no more than one *trendy* statement piece. The best *trendy* part is one of the "colors of the year" unless it is a neon hue. Go for sling-backs, pumps or *classic* sandals with a heel no higher than 2.5 inch (5 cm). They are easier on your feet when standing in line at the buffet. Have a cardigan in a color that matches the dress to cover up. At this time a year, it actually is still too cold for the dress you will wear when you live in a climate region with cold winters. You also need the cardigan to stay warm outside as you want to wear a light transitional coat. Wearing a winter coat with spring/summer shoes looks plain ridiculous. Remember, you don't want to be the family's "fashion victim".

Steer away from any solid color dress in pastels. You don't want to look like a walking Easter egg! When you like pastel colors, go for a skirt and top and add at least one non-pastel color (**Outfit 3.5**). A sheath dress with a print dominated by pastels is another option (**Outfit 3.6**).

Outfit 3.5. Easter skirt shirt look   **Outfit 3.6**. Easter look w. sheath

3.4 Mother's Day

On Mother's Day, women are in the center of the holiday. Mother's Day calls for a *girly* to *lady-like* look. Here are tips to create awesome outfits that suit everything from brunch to a family lunch or dinner including a family reunion in Mom's honor (see also **Section 2.1** Family Reunion).

When you are the daughter, avoid dressing against your *Mom's fashion rules* as she might feel offended. You want a peaceful day. When you are the mother, who is in the center of the party, avoid to dress like a matron. It will make you look *Old Lady*. Also avoid to dress like a cartoon book granny with bows, little floral prints, lace, lace-up booties, metal-frame round glasses, and a top-knot up-do all in one outfit. Such a look is ridiculous at any age, even at a Halloween party (**Section 3.8**).

Instead go for fun prints (**Outfits 2.7, 2.8, 3.6**) and cute cuts like fit-and-flare dresses (**Outfits 3.7, 3.8**) or blouses with Peter Pan collar. Add a playful bag and *fashion-forward* accessories. Pick friendly bright or pastel colors. It's spring.

Stay away from anything *trendy* regarding your clothes as most likely photos will end up in a family album/folder. You don't want to be in the center of your (future) grandkids' amusement in decades to come (see **Section 2.1** Family Reunion).

Outfit 3.7. Mother's Day look

Outfit 3.8. Mother's Day look

Here are some outfit suggestions:

- Tailored leather bomber, floral print skirt, color matching top and pumps, neutral color day bag
- Floral cardigan, straight solid color top and skirt picking up colors of the cardigan, nude pumps
- Pink dress, light blue tailored denim jacket or cardigan, floral or nude pumps, statement necklace, neutral color bag

3.5 Father's Day

Father's Day asks for relaxed *casual* outfits (**Outfit 3.9**). When the party is at a certain venue like a golf court, BBQ (see **Section 2.8**), picnic (see

Section 2.9), restaurant or beach, go with the *dress code* of the venue. The same applies for a ball game (see **Section 4.6**). Dress in the colors of and cheer for his team even when you favor the other guys. It's his honor day.

When you have a sibling or more, they most likely will also be present on Father's Day. Thus, Father's Day becomes sort of a mini family reunion (see **Section 2.1**). Thus, watch what you wear.

Unless your Dad is a baby-boomer and wore his jeans still when they became distressed and even ripped, stay away from the *distressed style*. When you wear distressed jeans, don't tell him that you bought them that way.

Riot your closet for *classic* summer items (**Outfit 3.10**). When he didn't like your wearing pants when you were young, wear a summer dress and wedges. Here are some ideas for putting together a Father's Day outfit:

- Bermuda, tunic, short bead necklace, strappy flat sandals
- Ethnic summer midi dress, wedge espadrilles, dangle earrings, wood watch or bangles
- Striped shirt, skorts or shorts, canvas sneakers, baseball hat
- Little white dress, denim jacket, ballet flats
- Gray T-shirt, white jeans, sage or olive utility jacket, long beaded necklace, wedges

Outfit 3.9 Father's Day posh casual **Outfit 3.10**. Father's Day dressy casual

3.6 National Day

All national day parades or parties require to dress up in the national colors. Thus, you must not be an American to get something out of this section of the book. Just switch red, white and blue with your Nation's colors.

No matter what your nationality is, when it comes to dress in the national colors one may end up looking costumed. Here are six tips to avoid looking ridiculous when dressing with the spirit.

1. Stay away from ruffles as they are an element of costumes.
2. Stay away from shorts, socks, T-shirts, dresses, shoes, sunglasses, jewelry, hats, bikinis etc. with flag prints. These items are disrespectful.
3. Pick items in the national colors from your closet and create a *casual* tasteful outfit that you could imagine to wear on a normal weekend.
4. When you do not want to go full on with your national colors just leave one color out.
5. Add another color to your national colors.
6. Substitute one or all of your national colors with a color in a slightly different hue, but the same color scheme.

Outfit 3.11. Outfit in national colors   **Outfit 3.12**. Red-white-blue outfit

Take into account where you will go, what you will do, and how long you will be on your feet as well as what is in the weather forecast. When you are invited to celebrate the National Day at a dinner party in your national colors, create a dinner outfit in the national or similar colors (see

Section 2.6 Dinner Party). When the plan is to watch a parade, opt for footwear that is comfortable to stand and walk in. When you attend an open-air concert or other open-air performances create an outfit as described in **Section 4.9** Cold, Wet Weather, but in your nation's colors. Here are some outfit suggestions:

- Denim jacket, slip dress in national colors, espadrilles, cross-body bag
- Boyfriend jeans, striped polo shirt in national colors, old-school canvas sneakers, saddle bag
- Denim skirt, top in national colors, strappy sandals or ballet flats, hobo or shoulder bag
- Straight skirt, blazer and top in national colors, nude or animal print pumps for a celebration at a restaurant or dinner party

3.7 Oktoberfest

In America, Oktoberfest is often celebrated throughout entire October instead of being in sync with the original Münchener Oktoberfest. In the US, there are many local breweries that celebrate Oktoberfest with special brews and "German" food. Small communities that were founded by German immigrants also celebrate Oktoberfest.

When attending an Oktoberfest at a local brewery there is no need to wear a dirndl or lederhosen unless you are part of the entertainment team. In most breweries, casual clothes - read jeans and shirt with sports shoes or sandals - are fine. When in doubt, let the usual *dress code* of the place be your lead.

When Oktoberfest is a community event, wearing something related to the theme is appreciated. Traditionally, dirndls are full length (**Outfit 3.13**), but the hem of contemporary versions falls around the knee. If you have a dirndl, Hosentürle skirt (**Outfit 3.14**) or lederhosen in your closet, the event will be your opportunity to wear it. Otherwise shop your closet for pieces like a full skirt with a white blouse or gingham shirt. When you have a gingham shirt or dress with about 3/8 inch (~1 cm) large pattern go for it. This size of gingham is about the traditional size for "Karohemden" as the Germans call this pattern. Waist-long flower embroidered fitted or boxy knit or boiled wool jackets over a black or vertical stripe full skirt are other options. Mary Janes, charm silver jewelry and tan or embroidered saddle bags convey a German vibe as well.

You should avoid to wear anything that goes into "Heidi" territory like high braids or a short full skirt. When you have long hair, a braided up-do is a nice finish. Here some outfit suggestions:

- Full midi skirt, gingham shirt under a corsage vest, lace knee socks, low heel Mary Janes, saddle bag

- Gingham below-the-knee shirt dress, white knee-high lace socks, wide embroidered folklore belt, medium heel Mary Janes, tan saddle bag
- Puff-sleeve blouse, full skirt, medium heel Mary Janes, saddle bag
- Linen shirt dress, hunter green jacket, red belt, Mary Janes, silver charm bracelet or necklace, saddle bag

Outfit 3.13. Traditional dirndl   **Outfit 3.14**. Hosentürle skirt w. denim

3.8 Halloween

Most Halloween costumes are still too expensive even when they are only $19.95 and 50% off. Cheap costumes are looking cheap and often show every lump and bump. There is nothing worse than cheap fabrics in combination with bad sewing, fit and color. While a twenty something may get away with it, for us over 40 it screams "time's up." Who wants to look like Frankenstein's monster, Snow White's stepmother, or Dracula's mistress anyway?

Instead of spending money on a cheap costume that does not work, save the money, and create an awesome Halloween look from your own closet. My late mom never bought costumes for us girls. Instead, she made us to take a look at our closets to create a costume from items we already owned.

Ask yourself "what are the roots of this design" and take your costume inspiration from there. Also ask yourself "what could this item be with a slight (reversible) modification?" As a kid, I sewed gold foil circles on a baby-blue nightgown to be the *Star Dollar* of the fairy tale by the Grimm brothers.

Outfit 3.15. Episodic costume **Outfit 3.16**. Pirate suitable blazer

When going for episodic costumes (e.g. **Outfit 3.15**), skip dressing like the decade that you grew up in to avoid looking like you try to re-live your youth. When you once bought an ethnic outfit on vacation, take your chance to introduce others to the beautiful traditional clothing of the country you visited. Be aware that doing so is a delicate balancing act. Wear it in a respectful, educational way. For instance, the cute Hosentürle skirt (**Outfit 3.14**) with a puff-sleeve blouse (no low cleavage please) and (low) braids, white lace knee-high socks and Mary Janes make a German girl's *Sunday's best* look. High braids and large cleavage would be caricature and would put the outfit in disrespectful territory. When you have long blonde locks, add a motorcycle jacket, motorcycle boots, and black leather pants and be *Mrs. Beryl Swain* for a night. Here are further Halloween outfit suggestions to shop from your closet.

- High-low hem blazer (**Outfit 3.16**), plastic or carton sword, knee-high boots, capris or riding pants, scarf wrapped around the head for a pirate costume
- Layering mesh or tulle skirt, leotard, ballet flats, ballerina knot for a Prima Ballerina costume

- Sleeveless sheath LBD, pumps, lots of costume jewelry, black opera gloves, up-do for a Holly Golightly outfit à la Breakfast at Tiffany's
- Sheath dress styled à la Mad Man with hair blown out to the outside, matchy-match accessories (e.g. pearl earrings and matching pearl necklace, same color for the bag and shoes)

3.9 Thanksgiving

A suitable Thanksgiving outfit partly depends on your plans. If you spend Thanksgiving with friends and/or family at home watching football you will dress comfortable and more casual than when you meet with friends at a restaurant for dinner or when you go to a Thanksgiving brunch with the family. Some families gather for Thanksgiving at one of the family members' house. In this case, it is important to not out-dress the hostess. Depending on your plans read also **Sections 2.1** Family Reunion, **2.6** Sunday Brunch, **2.7** Dinner Party, and **3.10** Christmas as appropriate.

Here are tips for all festivities where (over-)eating is involved:

1. Stay away from anything tight or high-waisted as such clothes become uncomfortable when you eat too much. Moreover, you don't want to look pregnant in the photos.
2. Deep jewel tones and darker colors except for red give the illusion of being slimmer than you are.
3. Dark colors are more forgiving when someone including you spills food on your clothes.
4. Go for easy to wash clothes, because there is a high risk for spillage, especially in the presence of kids. Recall dry cleaning is expensive, time consuming and bad for the environment.
5. Since you will sit a long time, wear wrinkle-free fabrics to avoid to have wrinkled clothes in the family photos.
6. Accessories are your friend to wear comfortable clothes, but still look *stylish*. A scarf or statement necklace, earrings, and/or bangle, immediately dress up your outfit a notch.
7. Resist your love for arm parties as multiple bangles make noise. Elderly family members have already enough difficulties to follow a conversation with the background noise from other conversations.

3.9.1 Thanksgiving Football Invitation

A Thanksgiving invitation to watch football calls for a *casual* outfit. A chunky long turtleneck sweater with leggings and statement shoes are a minimalist outfit. A statement cable-knit sweater (**Outfit 3.17**) or Fair Isle sweater with dark wash or black stretch skinny jeans and loafers work too. Jeans and a twinset with a pendant necklace or pearls are *classic casual* options (**Outfit 3.18**).

Outfit 3.17. Casual Thanksgiving   **Outfit 3.18**. Casual Thanksgiving

3.9.2 Thanksgiving Brunch

You can't go wrong with a lightly dressed up version of the restaurants *dress code* or what is worn at the restaurant's Sunday brunch (see **Section 2.7**). When the restaurant is new to you, dark dress pants, a white button-down shirt and a cardigan or sweater are great options. Add a pop of color either with the sweater/cardigan, shoes or bag. A pendant necklace gives the finishing touch. Wear dress shoes when the weather allows. Otherwise opt for *dressy* booties. When you swap the pants for a straight or A-line skirt knee-high boots work in cold nasty weather. See **Outfits 2.2, 2.3, 2.6** and **2.27** for further inspirations.

3.9.3 Thanksgiving Family Dinner

Here let the traditions of your family be the lead. When it is the first time you attend a Thanksgiving dinner at this part of the family ask your spouse/significant other to see photos from the last Thanksgiving dinner. Take the outfit of the most stylish family member(s) as your bar for creating an outfit. When deciding on your outfit keep in mind that the first impression is important. Making a great first impression is also important when the family had grown due to marriage and/or when family members will introduce their significant others. In all cases, your goal is to dress to impress.

A LBD with statement accessories is never wrong. You can vary this theme with a black sheath or shift dress with silver, gold or sequin detailing. A little red lace dress always turns heads when styled with chandelier earrings and *classic* black pumps. A solid green or red dress in a simple cut looks awesome with statement heels like pumps with jewelry details, or gold or silver pumps. A brocade or sequin skirt with a sweater work in cold climate regions (**Outfits 3.19, 3.20**).

Outfit 3.19. Brocade skirt

Outfit 3.20. Sequin skirt, Fair Isle

3.10 Christmas
There are many clothes and accessories made especially for Christmas starting with Santa's reindeers printed on underwear and ending with the ugly Christmas sweater. Cheap Christmas clothes often look like what they are: cheap. Looking cheap, however, is an aging look, and not an *ageless style*.

Of course, some designer Christmas sweaters are pieces of art, i.e. they are statement pieces in a world of Christmas sweaters. However, no woman over 40 in her best mind would spend a paycheck on a designer item that she can only wear once or twice a year.

Unless you want to settle for the "cute funny granny/auntie", and become the amusement of future family reunions, you should avoid Christmas clothes like the plague. When you absolutely want to go for the cute funny look, search for a genius-kitschy item that is so kitschy that it is great again. For example, a Rudolph sweater with a battery powered light bulb as red nose. In this case, family members would remember the fun the kids had switching the nose bulb on and off. However, think about this twice.

A safe bet are outfits that pick up Christmas-associated colors. Break the *old-fashioned* rule not to wear white after Labor Day and wear white with green or red for a modern, *fashion-forward* Christmas look without Christmas clothes (e.g. **Outfit 1.15**). Any green and red work (**Outfits 2.24**, **3.21**, **3.22**), even adjacent colors. However, avoid to dress like "Mrs. Claus." Here are some outfit suggestions for a Christmas family party, brunch or dinner (see also **Sections 2.1**, **3.9.2**, **3.9.3**):

- Plaid dress, skirt or blazer to dress in the spirit of the season
- Black-white hounds tooth blazer, black skirt, red sweater
- Red skirt or pants with green sweater or vice versa

Note that in some regions of the US, wearing an all-black attire for Christmas is a fashion faux pas.

Outfit 3.21. Christmas colors   **Outfit 3.22**. Just w. the spirit

3.11 New Year's Eve

What to wear on New Year's Eve depends on your plans, your location, transportation and the weather. A strapless long evening gown with a little faux fur stole and strappy 4 inch (10 cm) heels in a blizzard in New York guarantees you to start the New Year with a cold even when it is only five blogs to the opera.

3.11.1 New Year's Eve Bar Hopping

Great New Year's Eve looks for bar hopping are jeans with sequin or embellished tops (**Outfit 3.23**). Wearing one metallic or shine item with neutrals also fits the bill (**Outfit 3.24**). Unless you live somewhere warm, take a coat. A trench coat works for nasty rainy weather, a down coat or shearling with boots are best at below freezing temperatures. Pack your dance shoes in a bag.

Outfit 3.23. Bar hopping   **Outfit 3.24**. Bar hopping

3.11.2 New Year's Eve at a Sports Bar

When you plan to watch the playoffs at a sports bar, your goal is to create a sportive outfit with a *dressy* twist. It should not overly expose skin to the cold and the views. The outfit should be *festive*, but go with the sport theme (**Outfit 3.25**). Keep accessories at minimum as sport and jewelry are not a match except in dance sports. Here are suggestions for an evening at a sports bar:

- Long-sleeve, button-down shirt, tight, *dressy* shorts, metallic sneakers
- Slim cut leather joggers, slouchy top or sweater, low-heel pumps
- Leggings, metallic sneakers, tunic or long chunky sweater
- Sports pants, long-sleeve top, blazer, booties
- Sport jacket, black knee-length skirt, pumps, T-shirt
- Baseball jacket, denim skirt, lace-up shoes or sneakers, T-shirt

Outfit 3.25. Sports bar   **Outfit 3.26**. Winter resort

3.11.3 New Year's Eve Dinner Party at a Winter Resort

When you make the reservation for a New Year's Eve dinner at a winter resort ask for the *dress code*. A *semi-formal dress code* asks for a cocktail dress. Keep in mind that many winter resorts have dining rooms with an open fire. One never knows where one will be seated. Close to the fire it may be comfortable or even too hot. Far away, it may be too chilly. To stay on the safe side add a little evening jacket in the vibe of the dress. Avoid a stole as it is difficult to keep a stole in place for thermal comfort while eating. Wear strappy, heeled sandals. When the party is at another resort, bring strappy sandals in a tote and check your boots with your coat at the coat clerk's. When there is no *dress code* for the party err on side of *glam casual* (**Outfit 3.26**).

Here are outfit suggestions to stay comfortable in a room with fireplace:

- Lace top under lace cocktail dress, T-strap pumps, satin clutch
- Cocktail dress, bolero, strappy heels, patent leather clutch
- Cocktail skirt, matching jacket and pumps, *dressy* top, nude or black clutch

3.11.4 New Year's Eve Dance Party at a Tropical Resort

New Year's Eve parties at a Tropical resort ask for dressing up. Since you are in a vacation resort, *formal* dresses are not expected. Any dress that cannot be mistaken for a beach cover-up and is clearly not for work either will be fine (**Outfits 2.9, 2.10, 2.13**). See **Section 2.3.1** Beach Wedding for ideas on dress and jewelry pairings, but replace the flats for heeled, dance suitable versions. You can also try a:

- Floral asymmetric hem dress, black clutch, leopard high heels, long earrings, cocktail ring
- Solid high-low hem dress, contrasting clutch, statement necklace, studs, bangle, patent leather strappy heels
- Dark solid color layered dress, statement belt, strappy or red or metallic heels, contrasting color clutch, cocktail ring, medium size earrings

4 EVENTS IN TOWN

4.1 First Friday

First Friday is a big thing in many towns every month. Local businesses invite artists to exhibit their new work at their stores. The business owners offer wine, and refreshments, as well as finger food. First Friday is a win-win for the businesses, artists and community alike.

When spending an evening on the town to walk (or drive) from one exhibition to the next, talk with artists, visitors and business owners, you will be on your feet a lot. Comfortable, but non-orthopedic and non-sport shoes are a must. Your outfit should show your own personal style in a sophisticated way. It is an art event meaning you have the opportunity with your outfit to showcase some of your own creativity as well. By no way, do you want to compete with the art, but you want to fit in, in a positive way.

When it comes to art and fashion, you can't go wrong with an all-black outfit. However, many attendees will dress exactly with this concept in mind. It is the easiest way to fit in.

When your goal is to express your own creativity go for an unexpected, but sophisticated look. There are various ways to do this. Instead of all-black go all dark brown or dark blue. Wear items out of their typical context like an elegant blazer with leather pants (**Outfit 4.1**). What about wearing an item in a different way than what it was designed for? I am not talking about wearing a tuxedo jacket with the buttons on the back like Céline Dion did at the 1999 Oscars. Such a look is ridiculous at any age.

For example, style the Hosentürle skirt (**Outfit 3.14**), which is a modern female version of the Bavarian Lederhosen, with a brown plaid blazer, brown tights, brown booties and a green sweater. The latter adds a pop of color to the otherwise neutral outfit. Try to wear a shirt as a jacket, a cardigan as a top, a trench coat instead of a tunic over leggings, a dress over pants, or sport pants with a blazer (**Outfit 4.2**) just to give some examples. A cumber band could be worn with a button-down shirt and wide pants instead of a belt, i.e. it permits going from the desk to the exhibition by touching up the makeup, and swapping the studs for chandeliers.

Another option is to go for unexpected color combinations. For instance, fuchsia plus chocolate brown are a classic combination rarely seen in the arts scene and hence it creates the individuality you want to don.

Outfit 4.1. First Friday casual

Outfit 4.2. First Friday posh

Here are further inspirations for individual style on First Friday:
- Blazer, leather skirt, interesting top, booties
- Dress, black tights, print scarf, platform shoes
- All black, layered colorful necklaces or a statement necklace
- Leather pants, sweater, statement belt
- Floral dress with loafers
- Pleated leather skirt, red blazer, floral top, leopard print kitten heels or pointy toe flats, glass necklace
- Brown monochromatic look with cable-knit dress and imprinted belt for different texture, tailored motorcycle jacket for different shine, belt, booties
- All black look in a contrast of shiny, smooth versus mate and structured with leather joggers, patent leather pumps, and black cable-knit sweater

- Fabric motorcycle jacket, leather pants, bracelets, snake low heel pumps, all in neutral colors

Independent of the choice of your outfit, a cross-body bag or wrist bag are best. You want your hands free for snacking, holding a glass, paging in the event catalog or just for signing up on an email or newsletter list. Always remember "You should be either a work of art or wear a work of art." – Oscar Wilde

4.2 Fashion Event

Like for First Friday (**Section 4.1**), the idea of showing your own creativity applies to dressing for a fashion event. Sure, wearing black jeans with a black polo-sweater and white sneakers styled with pushed up sleeves à la Isaac Mizrahi or a black suit à la Karl Lagerfeld or Kate Moss to a fashion event is a no-fail recipe. The same applies for a LBD (**Outfit 1.23**) with statement bag and/or pumps. But when you are the gal who likes to stick out of the crowd or when you are in the mood for something more daring, create a *fashionable* outfit with <u>one</u> statement piece and <u>one</u> *trendy* item or a mix of prints (**Outfit 4.3**). When it is still too cold to go to the event without outerwear, opt for a statement coat.

Outfit 4.3. Fashion event mixed prints   **Outfit 4.4**. Fashion event trendy

Here are some outfit inspirations:

- Skinny gray pants, distressed black sweater, gray pumps, sequin jacket

- Leather pencil skirt, tuxedo or men's shirt, Swarovski crystal necklace, suede or velvet pumps
- Fair Isle sweater, pencil leather skirt, slouchy boots, belt to create a waist
- Wool sweater over a sequin top, plaid skirt, tights, booties, floral print scarf accessorized with multiple strands of pearls
- Black sweater, full leather skirt, coin necklace worn as belt, tights, Mary Janes
- Plaid skirt, sequin top under sweater, lace-up booties
- Pencil skirt, camisole under semi-sheer top, denim or bomber jacket
- Sequin skirt or leggings, cable-knit or Fair Isle sweater in neutral colors, lace-up flat shoes
- Sequin jacket, khakis, snake print pumps, gray T-shirt

Enjoy the show and remember: Some of the pieces presented are only meant as exaggerations of the trend to be shown off by the models. Even they would not wear those pieces on the street! A fashion show is a show after all!

4.3 Clothes Shopping

When shopping for new clothes or just updating the wardrobe with a trend, it is important to have an outfit that can be quickly removed to try the pieces out. Fitting rooms are always a nightmare. In Europe, they are as small as a toilet stall. In the US, they are three times that size, but all hooks on the walls and the bench are full of the last gal's rejects and/or misfits.

Here are tips what to wear for a successful and hassle free shopping trip:
1. Before you hit the stores, think about what you intend to buy and dress accordingly. When you shop for a skirt, pants or a top, wearing a dress is not helpful. You can't assess how the new pants/skirt looks with a typical top of your wardrobe or what the top looks like when worn with your typical bottoms.
2. When shopping for pants keep in mind the heel height of the shoes that you plan to wear with the new pants. Have them at least in your shopping bag when their heels are too high for the mall.
3. Speaking of shoes – wear comfy well broken-in shoes. You don't want to have a collection of blisters at the end of the day. The shoes should also be easy to slip on or off. Recall you hate to wait forever in line to get into the fitting room. Lacing up boots or shoes just takes too much time. The next gal is already waiting.
4. Don't wear anything tight as dressing rooms are small.
5. When you go to a flea market, make sure that you wear items under which or over which you can try things on. For instance, a wide

skirt with a T-shirt allows you to try on pants underneath the skirt, and shirts, jackets, or sweaters over the T-shirt.

6. Only wear a dress when you are shopping for a jacket to go with that dress or when you are shopping for another dress.

7. Have your cell phone as your most important accessory on that day. Mirrors lie! In stores, they often have slimming mirrors and/or tinted mirrors. They give you a nice tanned look that you only have after coming home from vacation. Consequently, it is hard to judge whether a color and/or cut are flattering on you. Ask a friend or sales person to take photos from the front, back and side. Who on Earth would only see you from the front to begin with?

8. Go for a shoulder or cross-body bag to have your hands free for browsing. Avoid rucksacks and backpacks. They may hit other people in the face when you turn around.

Outfits 4.7 and 4.8 are suitable for shopping for pants, jeans or tops in summer. In winter, the logistic is more complicate. In the suggestions below, swap the jeans for black tights and a skirt and the suggested shoes for knee-high boots with side zipper when you want to buy a skirt.

- Motorcycle leather jacket, sweater, boyfriend jeans, pearls, belt, wedge booties with zipper, shoulder or cross-body bag
- Jeans, long sweater, pea coat, driving shoes, shoulder or cross-body bag

Outfit 4.7. Shopping for bottoms/tops   **Outfit 4.8.** Shopping for skirts

Just two fitting tips:

1. Try out typical movements that you will do in the new clothes. When I buy a new dress for Argentine tango dancing, for instance, I make typical steps outside. When people start starring I smile and explain why I do it and they understand. When, for instance, you want to buy a pencil skirt for work, sit down. If it rides up, it will be too tight. Sit down in jeans and take a selfie of your bum. When you can see the Y, look for another cut with a higher raise in the back than the one you just tried out.

2. When you shop for a winter coat in late summer or early fall, have a thick sweater or a blazer in your tote or take an item with you in the fitting room that represents what you typically wear under your coat. You want to make sure that the coat will not be too tight. The small air layer between your indoor clothes and the coat is a valuable insulation layer. If you squeeze into the coat, you will lose body heat fast and feel uncomfortable in no time.

4.4 Balls and Dance Events

Balls get most women excited. A ball re-awakes all our fantasies about being Cinderella that we had as little girls. The beautiful gown, being in the arms of the guy of our dreams, becoming rich, being important, you name it. Now your loved one invited you to a ball! This invitation puts up the excitement what to wear to make the evening a great success.

No matter what ball you attend, gather information about the *dress code*, environment, and organizer to wear the right outfit. See **Section 1.1** Job Interview, **Section 1.10** Fundraising Gala and **Section 3.11** New Year's Eve Dinner at a Winter Resort.

4.4.1 Military Ball

For a military ball consider the uniform your date will wear. If he is wearing a *formal uniform*, you should dress in *formal attire* too. This means your gown's hem should not be higher than your knee. Tea-length – just above the ankles, but lower than the claves – works well when you intend to dance a lot (**Outfit 2.15**). Trains are never a good idea for a ball due to the stepping hazards. Remember you walk backwards and in heels when on the dance floor. Slightly less than floor sweeping is the longest you should go (**Outfit 4.10**).

Never show too much skin at a military ball. Either an Angelina Jolie type slit, or a front (**Outfit 4.9**) or back cleavage (**Outfit 4.11**). A back cleavage should never reveal the Y. A front cleavage should never compete with that of J Lo in her green dress on the red carpet. I think you know which dress I am talking about!

Make sure your dress fits and allows you to sit down. Ignore the size tag. It is inside the gown – nobody can read it. You even can cut it out if you hate it! However, think twice before you do so. Cutting out labels and size tags decreases the chances for consigning.

Any color other than red, or black will be remembered. This means you can wear a gown in a statement color only once in the same crowd, for instance, the burgundy chartreuse or blue gowns shown in **Outfits 4.9** and **2.16**, respectively. However, I think this rule applies for every gown due to the cell-phone photos posted on social media.

Outfit 4.9. Gown w. statement colors   **Outfit 4.10**. Black gown w. cape

On the upside, military moves every two or three years, so you may consider going for *classic* gowns, watch your weight, and re-wear them at the military balls at the new post. Thus, you only need two or three gowns that you rotate and update with accessories. You also may consider swapping gowns with your girlfriends who wear the same size. On many posts, there are stores to consign gowns. Check them long before a ball comes up, and again shortly after a ball to get the pick at the litter.

Never go for a prom dress after you graduated from high school. They look cheap and make you look cheap too. Even worse, they may harm your guy's career as his partner seems to be cheap and/or on the *trashy* side. Instead, rent a dress, or be proactive by buying a gown when it is on sale even though there is no immediate ball coming up and/or by checking upper level consignment stores regularly. Another great source for beautiful, high quality used gowns are *formal* wedding stores. After their high quality gowns had been rented out for a certain number of events, these stores sell them for the price of a cheap prom gown.

Never wear new shoes that are not broken in. You can't enjoy the night when your feet hurt. Go for shoes with leather or suede soles. Ballroom social dance shoes are great options. Rubber soles resist twisting and sliding and cause knee pain. Make sure that your shoes have a heel cap in the back to hold your foot in place when twisting and twirling. Sling-back pumps and sandals are a recipe for injuring your ankles. When your date is not a great dancer make sure you have closed toe shoes. Heels of 2.5 inch (5 cm) are best for dancing. Unless you are an experienced dancer and you are used to dance with a 3.5 inch heel (~9 cm) or more don't go there.

Style your hair *festive*, but matching to the style of your gown. The same applies to your jewelry, clutch or evening bag as well as makeup. When your dress is *romantic*, go for a curly up-do, *romantic* makeup, chandeliers or pearl necklace or choker, and a simple or *romantic* evening bag. Note *romantic* doesn't mean heart-shaped! If your gown is *edgy*, a studded evening bag and *dramatic* makeup will work.

Outfit 4.11. Retro lace dress   **Outfit 4.12**. Formal gown tea-length

Avoid over-bling! When you wear long chandelier earrings, skip the necklace (**Outfit 4.11**). When your gown has sequins, pearls, and/or crystals, go for small earrings and non-embellished shoes (**Outfit 4.9**). Leopard is a risky choice for a military (or any) ball. When you absolutely have to do leopard, keep it small (shoes, clutch).

Here are some outfit suggestions:

- Burned velvet 50s style gown in tea-length, crystal embellished satin pumps, long crystal earrings, silver clutch
- Sleek black evening gown, cropped jacket, satin belt with crystal buckle, crystal and pearl drop earrings, silver dance shoes, patent leather black clutch
- Retro-inspired black lace evening gown with wide skirt and fitted top, pearl choker, large fake diamond studs, gold clutch, velvet pumps

4.4.2 Social Dance

The *dress code* for a social dance differs among dance communities and clubs. It depends on the location (night bar, sports bar, dance bar, café, dance hall) and time of the venue, type of dances and the age of the majority of the attendees.

As a rule of thumb, assume that the more *formal* the dance is, the more *formal* is the outfit. Typically, the attire for smooth dances is *modest*, conservative (**Outfit 4.14**), and more dressed up than at venues with swing dances. While at the former, short necklaces, short earrings or studs and medium high heels are common, heels and jewelry are a safety risk at the latter. At social dances with mostly Latin music, outfits typically err on the more *sexy* side (**Outfits 2.13**, **4.13**) with cleavage, slits, mini-skirts, and/or high heels.

To get it right the first time you attend a social dance at a new place, find out what the usual *dress code* is. Use the same concept as for job interviews (see **Section 1.1**) or meeting his family (**Section 2.1** Family Reunion, **Section 3.9** Thanksgiving) when deciding on your outfit: The first impression is important and it is better to be over- than underdressed.

Browse the club's or organizer's webpage for the recommended attire and/or a phone number to call. Take hints from photos of past events on their webpage or social media and work from there. Take a sneak peek when they have an event to see what they wear. Consider these general aspects:

1. Always wear dance shoes or shoes with leather sole. Rubber soles including sneakers hinder in turning and spinning, which may injure your ankles and/or knees.
2. Stay away from sleeveless shirts, halter tops or dresses, strapped or strapless dresses as a courtesy to the lead. Who wants to touch damp skin?
3. Don't wear several top layers. They make leading and following more difficult.
4. Baggy sleeves are a safety issue in Latin and swing dancing.
5. Stay away from statement jewelry and belt-buckles for swing

dancing because they can cause scratches and bruises or be caught in clothing.

6. Don't put your keys in the pockets of your jeans or pants.

For an afternoon dance tea, dresses, skirts and tops that are distinctly different from work and/or vacation/beach dresses. **Outfit 3.7** and without jacket **Outfit 3.8** would work for an afternoon dance tea. Here are some suggestions for a social ballroom dance event:

- Solid color dress fit-and-flare or full-skirt dress, nude, metallic or contrasting shoes, short necklace that matches the neckline, studs
- Floral print summer day-time dress, metallic heeled sandals, classic pearl necklace, studs
- A-line dark skirt, floral or bright colored blouse, black dance shoes, short earrings

Outfit 4.13. Early Latin Dance night   **Outfit 4.14**. Smooth dance at a bar

In a sports or Western bar, a dark pair of jeans with a plaid shirt, T-shirt or white button-down shirt are always appropriate. **Outfit 3.23** would work as a *glam* dressed up version in a Western bar. Western boats are great options for line dance and alike, but too heavy for ballroom dancing.

In night bars, the *dress code* often changes as time progresses. Early in the evening, outfits tend to be casual, while after mid-night, outfits tend towards date-night outfits with cleavage and high heels. Thus, take the start and end time as your hint when you cannot gather information about the usual attire of the event.

4.5 Winter Sports, Sled Dog or Iron Dog Race, etc.

In high latitudes and in high altitude mountainous terrain, watching winter sport outdoor competitions like ski-joring, sled-dog and iron-dog races, cross-country and downhill skiing require an outfit with good insulation. Your outfit should permit staying outside thru the time of the race, i.e. it should avoid to lose body heat too fast. At the same time, you want to avoid sweating as the evaporation of sweat leads to cooling.

Air is a bad conductor. Therefore, creating several layers with a thin air layer in between is a good strategy to stay warm. Of course, warm underwear, well insulating shoes, hat with ear coverage, gloves and mittens are must-haves. When your feet or hands get cold, you will get cold too. Wear wool socks as they can take up a lot of water naturally before feeling wet. Wear two pairs where the outer pair should be looser than the one closest to your feet. There should still be some room between the socks and the shoes to avoid heat loss by conduction. Wear thinner finger gloves under your mittens.

Outfit 4.15. Yukon Quest outfit   **Outfit 4.16**. Sport race outfit

Unless you plan to go somewhere after the race, focus on styling your outerwear and creating an outfit for outside. Since you are attending a race, you want to look *casual* and *active* as well. Think of your hat, gloves and scarf as accessories to an outfit that consists of your bottom, boots and the outwear as your top.

In cold weather, sporty fabrics, stripes and prints for the top with a beret, beanie or other wool hats plus Alaska style flannel lining jeans, sneakers or wedges are good choices to stay warm and comfy and look *sporty*. Think of former governor Sarah Palin on February 17, 2007 waving the checked flag at the finish line of the Tesoro Iron Dog snow-machine race on the Chena River in Fairbanks when the First Dude and his team mate Davies finished first place.

The following outfit suggestions serve you well when attending winter sport events when worn with long Johns, a long-sleeve thermal, and double socks:

- Alaska-style 16 oz jeans with flannel lining, flannel shirt, sweater, puffer jacket long enough to cover your bum, pom-pom hat, scarf, gloves under mittens
- Puffer pants plus puffer jacket or puffer overall, jeans, sweater, puffer gloves, wool scarf, trapper hat, bunny boots
- Jeans, puffer skirt, sweater over flannel shirt, puffer jacket, scarf worn under the jacket, long pom-pom hat, gloves under patterned wool mittens, Sorel boots
- Long shearling coat or shearling parka, wool pants, turtleneck sweater, trapper or aviator hat, shearling booties, shearling mittens
- 16 oz jeans with flannel lining, turtleneck wool sweater, Kuspak-style velvet parka with puffer lining for insulation, bead embroidered shearling mittens, shearling lined knee-high boots, faux fur hat
- Aleutian pilot shearling parka, 16 oz jeans with flannel lining, sweater, shearling booties, gloves under leather gloves, cashmere scarf worn under the parka, beanie, duck boots

4.6 Ball Sport Event

When you are a hardcore fan of a team you surely have their *uniform*. In this case, just throw it on, blend in. However, what do you wear when your best female friend got an extra ticket and invites you to a game or your kid, nephew, nice or grand-kid has a game that they want you to attend because you are in town? The appropriate look for a ball sport event depends on the answers to the following questions:

1. What kind of event do you go to?
2. Will it be indoors or outside? When the game is outside, what weather is in the forecast?
3. What are the colors of the team that you are supposed to cheer for?
4. Do you want to express your style or blend in with the fans.

When style is more important to you than the team's colors go for *casual sporty* pieces (**Outfit 3.17**), and make sure that you avoid the other team's colors, but have those of her/their team somewhere in your outfit.

Riot your closet for casual items in colors close to the team's colors. To blend in with the fans, a T-shirt/sweater plus jacket if needed in colors close to those of the team with jeans and sneakers will be a safe bet. For instance, if the team has cardinal red and white, red and off-white will be fine (**Outfit 4.18**). It's about the intend, not about the exact colors (see also **Section 3.6** National Day).

In case of an outside venue and warm weather, flat sandals, moccasins, or canvas sneakers are great footwear options. Jeans, Bermuda shorts, cargo pants or not too short cutoffs or denim skirts work as well. Go for thin cotton layers for your top as you don't know whether you will have a place in the shadow or the sun. You want to be able to adjust your outfit for thermal comfort.

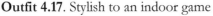

Outfit 4.17. Stylish to an indoor game   **Outfit 4.18**. Colors of the team

Speaking of the sun, bring sun screen, sunglasses, and a hat. A hat protects you from sunstroke. It should be flat and brimless on the sides to avoid blocking the view of the crowd behind you. When the game is in the evening, have a mosquito repellent. When you are allergic to pollen, spores and/or perfume, have medication handy. Also pack a bottle of water.

Go for a natural look with your makeup. When you have long hair go for a braid to protect your hair from being tangled. Recall that the friction due to the wind playing with your hair can cause split ends.

Things to avoid are anything body conscious, heels, a *fancy* up-do, bags that are not *casual*, the other team's colors, a mini-skirt, short shorts, or a short dress. Even style icon and designer of very body conscious dresses Victoria Beckham has been going *casual* when watching her husband's or kids' soccer games. And by no means wear mommy jeans!

4.7 Historical Parade

The New World's equivalent of the Hunters Parades, etc. are the parades hold in honor of a historic event like striking gold or founding a city. Of course, you can watch the parade in your usual weekend look. However, when you want to dress for the occasion or even have to marsh in the parade, but don't want to fork over the money for a costume, you can create a historic outfit from items in your closet (see **Section 3.7** Oktoberfest, **Section 3.8** Halloween). Search for pieces that have at least one prominent feature of the historical period plus minus a decade or two. Then combine these items in one outfit and fill in with classic pieces or pieces from even earlier decades. Make some reversible modifications as needed (see **Section 3.8** Halloween).

Outfit 4.19. Historic costume   **Outfit 4.20**. Historic outfit

Let's assume you have to dress for a time around 1900. At this time corsets were still a thing. Moreover, hats were big and statement pieces. Here are inspirations how to create outfits for that period:
- Tight vest/corset over white shirt with long full skirt (midi or tea-length work too), Russian scarf as stole, lace-up booties, wide brim straw hat accessorized with faux flowers and/or feathers from the

craft store

- Dirndl worn without apron or similar style dress, a wide belt, lace-up booties or oxfords, wool knee-high socks or tight, felt hat accessorized with faux feather and/or flowers
- Frock or duster, white button-down shirt, bolo tie, distressed jeans, hand-knitted wool socks, suspenders, brogues, wide brim hat, gold pan
- Silky fit-and-flare summer dress, cumber band, lace or long opera gloves, fishnets, Mary Janes, faux pony tail styled in an up-do with faux feathers, small velvet bucket bag

4.8 Open Air Concert

Summer is outdoor concert season. Concerts are to a certain degree an everything goes fashion wise. Thus, you may want to take a *fashion risk*, but err along your individual style to not go over board and to not look ridiculous.

When creating an outfit for an outdoor concert your goal is to look stylish, but also to be comfortable no matter what the weather is like. Here is some general advice. In the case of rain, go for wellies or rain booties, when the temperatures are below 70F (20°C). When they are above, wear flip flops to avoid sweaty feet. In the case of sun shine, canvas sneakers, flat strappy sandals, ballet flats, flat gladiators, or flat booties are suitable footwear. Which of these options is best depends the vibe of your outfit. Avoid footwear with high plateau soles because of the risk of ankle injury on uneven ground.

Sun screen and a hat are must-haves for protection from pre-mature aging (wrinkle and age-spot alert!). Since even the diffuse radiation in the shadow can cause a sunburn, reapply sun protection as directed. A hat keeps the sun out of your face. It can up your look when it matches the vibe of your outfit (e.g. floppy *Bohemian* hats, felt Western style, panama hats, wide-brim straw hats).

Bring an extra layer for chilly evenings. A button-down shirt in the vibe of your outfit or a *classic* jeans jacket will do. During the day knot the extra layer around the waist or neck. It looks stylish and you won't leave it somewhere. Stay away from anything knitted, lace or crocheted as the piece may get stuck in the chains of the person dancing/standing next to you.

Light-weight, breezy cotton fabrics are best. Dark floral and colorful ethnic prints are great for dresses, tops, pants or skirts. Plaid or lightweight denim shirts look awesome with jeans - and not too short shorts or cutoffs. Ethnic inspired dresses work well too.

Go for a cross-body mini-bag or belt bag. A large bag just jumps up and down when you dance and may cause bruises. A rucksack is risky when it is too large for the same reasons. Moreover, a rucksack may hit someone when you turn around. You are not used to moving with a hump like the Hunchback of Notre Dame.

Outfit 4.21. Outdoor concert dressy look **Outfit 4.22.** Concert casual look

While the twenty somethings look great with a romper, sandals, statement necklace, hat, and small cross-body bag, or short cutoffs, tank/T-shirt, fanny pack, sweatband and gladiator sandals, baby boomers and generation X may prefer a *Rock 'n Roll*, *Bohemian* or *punk* inspired style. Nice options for us over 40 are:

- Black harems pants with pockets, cotton top, long pendant necklace, silver thong sandals, belt bag
- Leather pants, striped top, denim jacket or vest, fabric cross-body bag, flat booties
- Ethnic/floral print cotton maxi dress, floppy or straw hat, short big wood beads necklace, flat leather sandals, cross-body mini-bag
- Ethnic cut inspired dress, denim shirt knotted around the waist, long pendant necklace, a leather Western inspired hat, flats or clogs
- Summer dress, floppy straw hat, mini cross-body bag, metallic thong sandals
- Wrapped shorts, T-shirt, chambray shirt knotted around the waist, Panama hat, strappy leather flat sandals or old school canvas sneakers, woven mini-bag
- Wide printed pants, solid color T-shirt, wide cotton scarf in

another print but matching colors that will serve as cover-up when it gets chilly, wide-brim straw hat, long pendant necklace, belt bag, flat leather sandals or slides

- Bell-bottoms, graphic T-shirt, espadrilles, floppy hat, flat oblong shoulder bag, all in a 21st century, not 70s vibe

4.9 Cold, Wet Weather

The wet and cold creep everywhere. The wind blows the rain or snowflakes into your face. As when the gray skies, gray streets, and nasty wind weren't enough, everyone at the tram station is dressed like they came just out of the coal mines. Gray and black everywhere, the umbrellas, coats, anoraks, scarves, gloves, bags, shoes, boots, ..., you name it. A typical winter day somewhere in mid-latitudes takes down everybody's mood. Everyone looks dull, annoyed and miserable. It seems like a new contagious virus.

Outfit 4.23. Coat with pops of red   **Outfit 4.24**. Cold weather gear

You can't change the weather. But you can dress to cheer your and others mood to make the day feel less miserable. Let's look at some basic facts first and then use them to dress for being comfortable in wet, cold weather.

It is important to understand that wind chills. Even though it may be just around freezing, the air feels much colder, the stronger the wind blows. Take this in mind when dressing!

Outfit 4.25. Shearling jacket w. skirt

Outfit 4.26. Poncho over coat

Outfit 4.27. Coat with belt, collar scarf

Outfit 4.28. Shearling coat w. hat

The closer the weave of a fabric is, the better it protects you from wind. My favorite fabric to keep the wind out is leather. It does not matter whether it is leather outerwear or leather as part of your indoor outfit worn under the outerwear.

A thin air layer is a great insulator. Thus, layering is key for thermal comfort in cold weather. For instance, a layering top under a sweater or jacket under your coat, tight or long Jones under your lined pants or jeans.

When it comes to protection from the cold, long is better than short. In this concept, boots are better than booties, long coats are better than short jackets, full-length sweaters are better than cropped tops, etc. If you hate the heavy weight of a long coat on your shoulders, you can go for a short coat or jacket plus insulating over-skirt.

Outfit 4.29. Shearling w. belted scarf   **Outfit 4.30**. Wrap scarf over coat

Recall the cold feather-beds when you slept in granny's attic during your childhood? Unless your feather puffer coat has a water repellent outer fabric, skip the idea to wear it in wet weather. Feathers take up humidity. The moisture evaporates due to your body heat and the evaporative cooling makes you feel cold in that down coat. In general, go for semi-permeable fabrics that let moisture go out, but not in. They let body moisture penetrate to the ambient air, but prohibit the moist ambient air to move inside. This concept protects from getting cold due to evaporating sweat.

Wearing bright colors makes you feel like a gold fish in a sea of herring. It makes you feel good when you enjoy to stand out style-wise (**Outfits 4.31, 4.32**). You can achieve the same effect by creating an interesting outfit with different structures. The secret behind this kind of outfits is that when everything seems to look the same the humans' eyes get bored. They start searching for something different. In the moment, the eyes fall on your outfit there is an unconscious glimpse of success in the onlooker's eyes. It makes them and you feel better than before at least for a moment. Mission accomplished. Here are further styling suggestions for outerwear:

- Red or other bright color pea coat, boyfriend jeans, heeled loafers or wedge sneakers, winter white hat, scarf, mittens
- Striped below-the-knee winter coat, head band, satchel bag, over-the-knee boots
- Long-sleeved T-shirt/layering top, flannel shirt, cardigan, winter coat, long leather gloves, leggings under lined leather pants, tightly woven scarf, wind-secure hat (beret, beanie, pompom hat), socks, booties
- Skinny jeans, over-the-knee booties, long-sleeve T-shirt under cable-knit sweater, long coat, scarf, hat, gloves, saddle bag
- Two pair of tights, skirt, boots turtleneck sweater under blazer under a long coat, gloves, hat
- Leopard print jacket, wool pants, matching booties, burgundy beret, fuchsia bag
- Pants/jeans, bright color short insulating skirt, winter jacket, booties, beret or pompom hat, bag

Outfit 4.31. Trench coat w. umbrella

Outfit 4.32. Classic trench coat

5 REFERENCES

While most of the outfits shown here were styled using clothes that I bought myself, the following items are samples of my choice that I received courtesy of the following brands:

Akoya saltwater pearl necklace c/o The Pearl Source
Striped black skirt c/o eShakti
Wood watches c/o Jord
Boot toppers c/o Top of the Boots
Trench coat, asymmetric blazer, dresses c/o Lookbook Store
Striped T-shirt c/o Marine Layer
Green T-shirt c/o ONNO
Tights and leggings c/o No nonsense
Tight c/o Hanes Hosiery
Leggings c/o Red Bubble
Black and white jade necklace c/o Almo Jewellery
Layering top c/o Adea
Summer dress c/o HSN
Summer dress c/o Needham Lane
Work dress c/o Ronen Chen
Slides c/o Vionic shoes
Jacket c/o London Tradition
Haftee c/o Halftee
Straw and pleather bag c/o Olivia and Joy
Sundress c/o Tropical Hawaiian Apparel
Musse & Cloud sandals c/o Coolway

ABOUT THE AUTHOR

Nicole Mölders, 54, is a fashion, science and dance enthusiast living with her husband and cat near Fairbanks, Alaska. She is the blogger of *High Latitude Style* – an Alaska fashion blog with science bits for stylish women in midlife. She is also a professor at the University of Fairbanks Alaska teaching atmospheric sciences and pursuing research on human and natural impacts on weather and air quality as well as on the physics of clothes. She is the author of *Land-use and Land-cover Changes – Impacts on Climate and Air Quality*. She also co-authored a textbook entitled *Lectures in Meteorology* with Gerhard Kramm.

Grown up in Europe, where she lived in France and Germany, her style is a mix of *Euro Chic* and *American Classic*. Think along the line of Emmanuelle Alt and Kate Moss with a bit of Lauren Hutton, Grace Kelly, and a lot of Jackie Kennedy, and some Jackie Onassis. She loves classic denim jackets, leather aviator and motorcycle jackets, cashmere cardigans with sleek sheaths, or shirt dresses, pencil or straight skirts with cashmere sweaters or twinsets. Being an avid dancer fit-and-flare dresses and gowns are in the mix as are studs and pearls.

Living in Interior Alaska since 2001 where temperatures can be below freezing for seven to eight months a year, has made her an expert at stylish layering for insulation and styling outerwear.

She is regularly invited by various women groups in Alaska to talk about fashion and style. Among other subjects, she gave talks on the physics of clothes, about fashion history, and how to dress for success.

Being an educator, she explains in this fashion and style book, why an outfit works or doesn't, how to create ageless outfits, which aspects to consider when dressing for an occasion, and what to avoid when composing an outfit and why.

In this book, she focusses on *How to Dress for Success in Midlife* and encourages women to re-invent themselves for their best style ever.

You can find her on
Facebook at https://www.facebook.com/HighLatitudeStyle, Google+ at https://www.google/+Highlatitudestyle,
Pinterest at https://www.pinterest.com/HighLatitudeSty,
Twitter @HighLatitudeSty,
Instagram @highlatitudestyle and on her blog *High Latitude Style* at

https://www.highlatitudestyle.com

Printed in Great Britain
by Amazon

27911069R00064